Joel and

Also in this series by Ellen Cheshire

Jane Campion
Ang Lee
Audrey Hepburn

Also in this series by John Ashbrook

Brian de Palma
Terry Gilliam

Joel and Ethan Coen

Ellen Cheshire
and John Ashbrook

www.pocketessentials.com

This edition published in 2005 by Pocket Essentials
P.O. Box 394, Harpenden, Herts, AL5 1XJ
www.pocketessentials.com

Distributed in the USA by Trafalgar Square Publishing,
P.O. Box 257, Howe Hill Road, North Pomfret, Vermont 05053,

A CIP catalogue record for this book is available from the British Library.

ISBN 1 904048 39 0

2 4 6 8 10 9 7 5 3 1

Typeset by Avocet Typeset, Chilton, Aylesbury, Bucks
Printed and bound in Great Britain by Cox & Wyman, Reading

Dedications

Whenever I read a book of any kind, I am always intrigued by the author's dedication and acknowledgements. I wonder, who are these people, and what importance do they play in the author's work or life? Well, in the four Pocket Essential books I've written I've managed to dedicate a book to all my close family – so this revised Third Edition I'm going to dedicate to the memory of my grandma 'Danny' who sadly passed away last year. – *Ellen*

Well, if we're being all maudlin about it – I'll dedicate my bits to my grandparents as well. My granny died when I was still at college, before I'd done any of the interesting things I've spent my adulthood doing in lieu of work. She never heard me on the radio. Never saw my name on the cover of a book. Thing is, she was enormously proud of me anyway. I guess families are like that. – *John*

'He told them to look not at the facts but at the meaning of the facts, and then he said the facts had no meaning.'

Contents

CONTENTS

Preface to the Third Edition: Now That the Marriage is Winding Down.

When we first wrote this book, we found that half of the battle was not deciding what to *put in*, but what to *leave out*. To decide what is, and is not, 'essential.' When we came to this revised edition, although we had more pages, thanks to a larger typeface (well, we're all getting older... the eyesight isn't what it was) we had no more words, yet four more films and a few odds and ends to fit in. Easiest thing in the world. We just had to decide what to *take* out.

The preface was the first thing to go. So, without further...

Brothers Coen: You're Exposed.

The Brothers Coen are a phenomenon. Not since Groucho, Chico, Harpo and the one everyone forgets, have Brothers made such an impact on popular culture. The Wachowskis, Wayanses, Blueses, Smothers and Karamazovs all owe their success to the pioneering work done by The Coens. Obviously.

Sharing the writing, producing and directing chores on their films ensures that the Coen siblings' vision gets to the screen in as undiluted a manner as possible. And it is a vision which has, for more than two decades, led the vanguard in American independent film-making.

Now, the fact that their films are often funny makes some commentators believe the Coens have nothing to say; whilst others believe that the films are so packed full of significance that the comedy is merely a distraction. As with most things Coenical, there is merit in both of these positions, despite the seeming coentradiction.

And yes, we'll continue to use these bad typographical puns until we get bored of them. Don't hold your breath.

Although allegations of auteurism have frequently been levelled at them, the Brothers Coen are, in fact, aggressively collaborative. Much of the pleasure derived from a Coen film comes from the contributions of their regular ensemble of actors and technicians.

However, it is true that they discourage improvisation on

set, because their scripts are so carefully and completely written that any changes can shift the balance within a story. In his article 'The Brothers From Another Planet', David Handelman sat in while the Coens wrote *Raising Arizona*. Ethan did the typing and smoking whilst Joel did the pacing and smoking. They mooched around Joel's apartment, talking ideas through before committing them to paper. 'The Coens write scripts without an outline, painting themselves in and out of corners "Wildy style." According to Joel, Mack Sennett's silent film studio employed certified lunatics called Wildies, who would come to script meetings and blurt out crazy, non-sequitur plot ideas, which Sennett would often use.' How terribly liberating. Of course, it could be nonsense they made up just to tell journalists. The Coens are defiantly unreliable interviewees, maintaining an image of bumbling good-humoured amateurism, which their films consistently confound.

Joel and Ethan were born in St Louis Park in Minnesota on 29 November 1955 and 21 September 1958, respectively. Their parents were Edward, a professor of economics, and Rena, an art historian and university teacher. They spent much of their childhood together; shooting Super8 remakes of feature films. In his book *The Making of The Big Lebowski*, William Preston Robertson talks very movingly about their reinterpretation of 1943's *Lassie Come Home* as the slightly more straightforward *Ed... A Dog*.

Still, given their parentage, they really had to put aside such childish things and get a degree or two. Joel took Film at New York University before finishing his graduate studies at the University of Texas at Austin. Ethan had to make do with reading Philosophy at Princeton. During his final year, he also fulfilled a lifelong ambition to work as a statistical typist at Macy's department store. To this day, he is still the typist in the family.

Both brothers married and divorced early, then remarried: Ethan to film editor Tricia Cooke; Joel to actress Frances McDormand.

The films of the Brothers Coen don't usually make much profit, but the critics love them, awarding bodies admire them and the cream of Hollywood actors want to be in them. Working, more often than not, within the tight confines of the crime genre the Brothers Coen have still managed to create a unique vision of an odd universe at a tangent to ours. The world according to the Coens is a great place to visit, but don't lose sight of the way home.

Before we go there, a few words about a strange local custom: In the cast and crew credits for each film, you will encounter the occasional superscript numeral, for example Frances McDormand[1]. These numbers will clock up throughout the book, as the Coens' various collaborators return to the fold again and again. See if you can guess who will have the highest number after their name by the end of the book. It's a fun game for all the family especially, you know, for kids!

Blood Simple (1983)
'The world is full of complainers'

Cast: John Getz (Ray), Frances McDormand[1] (Abby), Dan Hedaya (Marty), Samm-Art Williams (Meurice), M Emmet Walsh[1] (Visser), Deborah Neumann (Debra), Holly Hunter[1] (Helene Trend's voice on Meurice's answer-phone)

Crew: Director: Joel Coen, Producer: Ethan Coen, Writers: Joel & Ethan Coen, Cinematographer: Barry Sonnenfeld[1], Music: Carter Burwell[1] & Jim Roberge, Editors: Roderick Jaynes[1] & Don Wiegmann, Colour, 100 minutes

Plot: Abby is the young wife of Julian Marty and the illicit lover of Ray. Marty is not best pleased by this so he hires sleazy private dick Visser to murder Abby and Ray in their adulterous bed. Instead of actually doing this, Visser takes the money and shoots Marty, using Abby's gun, which he leaves lying around to ensure that she gets the blame for her husband's death. Unfortunately, he also leaves his engraved cigarette lighter behind!

Commentary: *Blood Simple* was the Brothers Coen's feature film debut and, by combining a narrative quite unlike anything mainstream Hollywood was producing at the time, a script as dense as a novel yet as purely entertaining as a B-movie pot-boiler, and a confidence far beyond their tender years, it firmly established Joel and Ethan as big-time players in the American independent film world.

It also marks the first of three cinematographic outings Barry Sonnenfeld made with them, before forging a successful Hollywood directing career of his own (*The Addams Family*, *Get Shorty*, *Men in Black*). Involved from the start, he was the cinematographer for the three-minute teaser trailer they shot to help secure funding. Working with Joel and Ethan to create the storyboards, he was instrumental in creating many of the high-contrast lighting effects which reflect the mood of the characters.

In an interview in *Film Comment*, the Coens insist to Hal Hinson that they, 'didn't want to make a Venetian blind kind of [detective] movie.' And yet, how is Ray's bungalow lit? Chilly sunlight streaming in through Venetian blinds in every room. And Marty's office? The same. Throughout the film, prison-bar shadows cross walls, floors and ceilings, as well as sleeping lovers and the dying bar owner.

When Ray and Abby repair to bed, the drone of passing cars and the panning of headlights accompany their humping. Already we have established that light is precious and what little there is of it punches temporary holes through the darkness. Like the flashbulb of a camera. Maybe Abby is attracted to Ray because of his name; maybe she needs him to be her Ray of Light.

Where *Fargo* uses white to bleach out detail and hide the horizon, leaving the characters disconnected from the outside world (as, for that matter, does Sam Raimi's 1998 take on the familial betrayal theme, *A Simple Plan*) *Blood Simple* uses deep, endless dark to the same end. Colour, when it arrives, is muted and consigned mostly to vulgar neon signs.

Sonnenfeld's cameras were pushed to their limit. In such light, even modern fast films tend to look grainy, and the

Coens exploit this here. Films don't come much darker than this. James Foley's 1985 rural nihilistic nightmare *At Close Range* is one. Kathryn Bigelow's 1987 trailer-trash vampire movie *Near Dark* another. Both are about the self-destruction of unlovely families set against a murky and cold rural backdrop. So, no similarity to *Blood Simple* at all then.

One of the reasons the film remains fresh is that its influences are not only from hard-boiled crime fiction. Its low-key lighting and gruesomely comic silent sequences owe a great debt to the modern American horror movie, particularly George Romero's *Night of the Living Dead* (1969) and Sam Raimi's *The Evil Dead* (1982).

This horror element, coupled with an imaginative reworking of the standard murder-mystery thriller genre, created what was to become a template for subsequent Coen films: take a standard genre and manipulate it until it becomes something unique – a film which is a cross between an affectionate homage, a cheeky pastiche and an original piece of film-making.

As with those original detective yarns from the 1940s, *Blood Simple* opens with a narration that sagely informs us: 'The world is full of complainers. But the fact is, nothing comes with a guarantee.' (Time has proven this to be just as true of Coen films.) This is played out against images of a long, straight road surrounded by flat, featureless wasteland; which becomes the film's central metaphor – these characters are travelling alone with no destination in sight.

The grass-roots seer in question is the private dick, Loren Visser. In itself, it is not unusual for the detective to narrate a crime story. It's a little more unusual for him to be the bad guy and even less usual for him to be dead. Those crazy Coens. Although he wears the white Stetson, he certainly isn't the good guy. There aren't any good guys in this murky world.

The narration continues: '...what I know about is Texas... and down here... you're on your own.' This is only true in an existentialist sense. If you live in a Godless universe then you can do as you will. Although it may be nothing we would recognise as God – something is working behind the scenes to ensure that bitter irony will confound the best-laid plans, and arrange something remotely resembling justice. This too will become a common Coen theme.

As the opening credits roll across the lovers' rain-lashed windscreen, interspersed with oncoming headlights like flashes of thunder, Abby tells Ray of her marital problems. He, in turn, confesses that he has always 'liked her.' Seemingly safe and dry inside their car, their conversation wanders into dangerous territory.

Rain is often used to symbolise high passions and here works as an aphrodisiac. This drive through the dark is also deliberately reminiscent of the opening moments of Robert Aldrich's *Kiss Me Deadly* (1955) and Janet Leigh's flight from justice to the Bates Motel in *Psycho* (1960). This particular reference is underlined as Abby suggests they stop at a motel for some sex.

Interestingly, she only does this after she confirms that there is a car (Visser's Volkswagen) following them. Is she drawing Ray into her web, to set him up as the patsy for some future crime against her husband, or does she genuinely desire him?

The failure of Abby's relationships with her husband and Ray is brought about by an inability to communicate yet, when she is in the car with him, Abby foists intimate details of her marriage onto Ray despite his repeated protestations that he is, 'not a marriage counsellor.'

Later, after Ray and Abby have set up home together, Ray goes to Marty and asks for money. This is one of the few scenes where Marty talks of his relationship with Abby and warns Ray of her expensive tastes. When Ray protests, Marty snaps back, 'What're you, a fucking marriage counsellor?' This links the two men, fatally.

Ray's confrontation with Marty, as he sits on the stoop, glaring at the billowing, roaring incinerator, is the beginning of Marty's terrifying revenge, his rebuilding of his battered pride. This incinerator and the overhead fan in his office, provide the soundtrack to Marty's life as he grumbles that he is, '...right here in Hell.' This will not be the last time a Coen film makes a glancing reference to the afterlife.

All in all, Marty doesn't say much in the film – indeed, on a number of occasions he is seen leaning back in his office chair, beneath the large fan, thinking. The first time we see this idiomatic pose is when Meurice (another bartender) enters the office and comments, 'I thought you were dead.' Later, when Ray enters and sees that pose, he comments, 'I thought you were deaf.' The irony is that by this point Marty is actually dead.

That large overhead fan has a twin in Ray's apartment. Both are constantly in use, indicative of extreme temperatures and providing a thumping heartbeat that masks what little dialogue there is. They also fuel confusion and misunderstanding. For instance, the steady thump in the background of an otherwise silent phone-call acts like a signature for Marty (even after he is dead and in the ground and, presumably, really in Hell), convincing Abby that he is still alive, because the call is clearly coming from his office. It isn't. It's Visser calling from Ray's home, sitting beneath his fan. This mechanical heartbeat also links Marty and Abby. The dissolve from Marty staring up at his fan to Abby staring up at hers is a cunning visual clue to the link that still exists between man and wife.

There are many instances throughout this film where man-made machines groan with an ominous, dissatisfied ache. Like the gas pipes in David Lynch's *Eraserhead* (1976) and *The Elephant Man* (1980), but also like the breath that whistles down the corridors of the hotel in *Barton Fink* and the swishing of the giant clock on the exterior of The Hudsucker Building.

One suspects that a driving motive for the Coens to remix the film into 1998's *Blood Simple: Forever Young* was the chance to employ some of their sound experiences from their later films into upgrading the sound to stereo, thereby making all of this experimentation with sound all the more impressive.

When Marty breaks into the bungalow and tries to take Abby back by force, she frees herself by breaking his index finger and kicking him in the *cojones*. It is only when Marty is on the floor vomiting that Ray comes limply to the rescue. Not only has Marty been defeated but he was defeated by a woman and humiliated in front of her new lover. It doesn't require Sigmund Freud to work out that the breaking of his 'pussy finger' can be seen as a form of castration.

Of course, evoking Freud may seem unnecessarily pretentious at this point but it is invited – the subject is raised within one of the film's few comedy asides, when Abby announces that she had been to a psychiatrist who had diagnosed her as '...the healthiest person he ever met,' whilst Marty was 'anal in the head.'

So, considering his anal head and his castrated finger, he really only has but one course of action left to him: revenge. Re-enter Visser. He passes Marty the obviously doctored photographs, 'evidence' of the execution and for a moment fools us into thinking that maybe he is too moral to kill the innocent couple and will just rob Marty.

Wanting to keep the photo Marty surreptitiously swaps it for a not-inappropriate 'Now Wash Your Hands' notice, before paying the cackling Visser. Then, as if being metaphorically castrated by Abby weren't enough, Marty is finished off by the ultimate sexual indignity – he is shot with his wife's little gun.

'Look who's stupid now!' gloats Visser, walking away leaving his inscribed lighter hidden beneath the pile of recently caught fish. This lighter, which causes much consternation for the film's second half, remains undiscovered and can therefore be considered a red herring.

When Ray arrives, the red light on the ceiling (presumably the glow from the incinerator flame) is mirrored by the red of the blood on the floor. This is the first and only time red plays any significant part in the film. When he finds Abby's pearl-handled pistol, he makes the connection Visser hoped for and proceeds to dispose of his body and all the evidence.

With Marty leaking on the back seat, Ray leaves civilisation behind him and sets off down that long, straight, doomed highway. It is the same symbolic highway which runs through Hitchcock's *North By Northwest* (1959), Lynch's *Lost Highway* (1996) and, not coincidentally, through *Raising Arizona*, *Miller's Crossing*, *Fargo* and *O Brother, Where Art Thou?* as Ray proceeds through the night, down this road, the radio evangelist is preaching the Apocalypse. Just what you want to hear when you've got your boss cooling on the back seat and a spade in the boot. Of course, one of the more user-friendly chapters of The Bible – 'Revelations' – tells us that, come the Apocalypse, among other delights, we can look forward to the dead walking again.

Cue Marty to start moaning and squirming in the dark. Ray panics and abandons the car for a moment. When he returns, the back seat is empty. Marty is crawling along the road, silhouetted by the headlights in a moment chillingly reminiscent of Romero's *Night of the Living Dead*.

And so it is out here, in the quite literal middle of

nowhere, that Ray will face his severest moral test, a test than runs through the core of most Coen movies: just how far is he prepared to go to get what he wants?

Finally, resigned to the horror of it all, Ray decides to bury the body in a freshly ploughed field, and begins digging a hole. Marty, still conscious, points Abby's gun at Ray but it is empty. Even in death, he cannot escape Abby's emasculation. Ray takes the gun and does the indecent thing, burying Marty whilst he is still squirming and howling.

The morning after the night before is cold and stark. The sun doesn't rise and shine on this side of Texas – it just chases the dark away so Ray can see the full horror of what he has done. We see an overhead shot of Ray's white car, stranded in a dark sea of soil. As a final act of disrespect, Ray drives over Marty's grave.

Abby's apartment is emblematic of the personality of all four main players: empty. She only has one ornament – a piggy bank. There are no carpets, no curtains, nothing to make the house a home. This motif reappeared in Steven Soderbergh's *sex, lies and videotape* (1989), where the moral vacuum of the characters is represented by big, hollow houses. Ray is revealed sitting in her chair – one of Abby's few pieces of furniture – with his cowboy boots on the table, mirroring Marty's earlier pose.

When Abby answers the phone, in her overwrought state, she mistakes Visser for Marty (thanks to that overhead fan) and mistakenly confirms that he is still alive. This enrages Ray, who is rapidly reaching the end of his tether. The last time anyone saw Marty, he was still squirming. This implants a thought in Ray's mind, and the viewers': 'maybe Marty isn't dead, maybe he's coming back for revenge.'

Meanwhile, the real threat is Visser, still out there in the dark, hunting for his missing photograph and lighter. In the hollow auditorium of Abby's cold house, Ray's transformation into Marty becomes complete when he echoes Marty with the words, 'You're just saying that [you love me] because you're scared!' It is appropriate then, that this is the moment Visser kills him too.

Ironically, it is Abby's lack of house-pride (or, more precisely, her lack of curtains) which gets poor, dumb Ray killed. This murder starts off relatively cleanly – shot from a distance by a high-powered rifle – then gets very nasty as Visser finishes him off with the piggy bank.

At this moment, the film turns into a stalk 'n' slash movie as Visser hunts Abby through scenes lifted from *Halloween* (1978). In the dark, she can't see Visser and, because she has been haunted by the nightmare of Marty's return, believes that her attacker is actually her husband.

When he is caught on the far side of the bathroom wall, Visser fires indiscriminately through the wall into the pitch-black room beyond. Significantly, these holes punch beams of harsh light into the dark – visually tying this situation to the opening scenes' introduction of the lovers and the previous night's burial scene.

Visser is now, unwittingly, Abby's next victim. In Abby's mind, they have all become Marty. For an allegedly psychologically healthy person, she seems chewed up by guilt.

The most chilling aspect of this cat-and-mouse finale is the tragic confusion of it all. Abby never knows who the 'cat' is, nor why he is trying to kill her. Visser, in turn, is mistakenly convinced that she knows who he is and what he's done.

As she shoots at the shadowy figure behind the door, she calls out, 'I'm not afraid of you Marty.' Visser ends his days laughing good-naturedly at the irony of his and Abby's mistakes – and gazing in fascination and horror at a water droplet which is hovering on the brink of dropping... much as his life is.

As the credits roll, the strains of 'Same Old Song' by the

Four Tops play us out, indicating that everything has been seen before, no one learns from the past and that irony is alive and well, and living in Texas. So don't complain.

Families: There are no classic American nuclear family units presented here. The only images of happy people we see are the black and white photographs lining the walls of Abby and Marty's home. Ray constantly looks at one in particular, of them in beachwear.

If you feel the need to impress your A Level Film Studies lecturer, you can always pull a little Freud out of your hat: Ray and Meurice can be seen as spiritual sons to Marty. They help run his bar and are entrusted with a certain amount of responsibility and security. Therefore, there can be an Oedipal reading of the film, where Ray (the son) looks longingly at the happy photograph of Mom and Pop, and decides to take Pop's place. This he does, and in the process loses the respect and friendship of his brother, Meurice.

The contrast between the two sons is made more obvious through the casting of black actor, Samm-Art Williams as Meurice, and blonde-haired, blue-eyed John Getz as Ray. Working against racial stereotypes, it is Meurice who is the good loyal son, and Ray that turns out to be deceitful and ultimately a killer.

Dreams: In Abby's dream sequence she walks into her darkened living room. The light from the open bathroom door reveals Marty sitting on her bed (a position Ray is in when Abby returns to her apartment during the film's final showdown). He throws her compact to her, repeating Ray's phrase, 'You left your weapon behind.' This is a manifestation of her guilt and an unsubtle indication that in the Film Noir genre men use guns to inflict harm whilst women use guile and a lot of make-up.

Blood Simple: Forever Young (1998)

Additional Cast: Jim Piddock, Kenneth Loring.

Additional Crew: Commentary written by: Joel and Ethan Coen.

As part of the belated reassessment of the Brothers' earlier works, *Blood Simple* has now been recut, remastered, remixed into stereo and rereleased. Characteristically bucking the trend, when the Brothers Coen release a Director's Cut it is actually one whole minute shorter than the original. Joel claims that this is because he 'cut out all the boring bits.'

The American Region 1 DVD released in 2001 features a spoof introduction by Mortimer Young of 'Forever Young Film Preservation' and an audio commentary by the no-less impressive Kenneth Loring.

If the Internet news groups are anything to go by, this commentary is universally despised by American fans. It's not hard to see why. Mr Loring is English, therefore his accent and idioms may have proven difficult for the typical American consumer. But the problems run deeper than that. Basically, the Coens have taken a great deal of time and trouble in deliberately antagonising their fan-base.

There are noticeable differences between this and the generally available video version: The song 'Sugar Pie Honey Bun' has been removed and 'I'm A Believer' reinstated, as was originally heard in the cinema release, then removed from the video for copyright reasons. More troubling is the virtual disappearance of Samm-Art Williams. His already occasional appearances have now been noticeably trimmed.

Smoothing out the odd continuity bump and trimming the edges make little appreciable difference to the film, but it's a delight to finally see it in its proper widescreen ratio with the added clarity of a DVD picture. Be warned, however, the extras are really only for hardened fans.

Crimewave (1985)

a.k.a. *The XYZ Murders /*
Broken Hearts and Noses

Cast: Reed Birney (Vic Ajax), Louise Lasser (Helene Trend), Paul L Smith (Faron Crush), Brion James (Arthur Coddish), Sheree J Wilson (Nancy), Edward R Pressman (Ernest Trend), Bruce Campbell[1] (Renaldo 'The Heel'), Frances McDormand[2] (Nun), Joel Coen (Reporter at Execution)

Crew: Director: Sam Raimi[1], Producers: Bruce Campbell, Cary Glieberman, Edward R Pressman, Irvin Shapiro, Robert G Tapert, Writers: Ethan Coen, Joel Coen & Sam Raimi, Cinematographer: Robert Primes, Music: Joseph LoDuca & Arlon Ober, Editors: Michael Kelly & Kathie Weaver, Colour, 86 minutes

Plot: Simple but kind security system installer Vic Ajax works for the diminutive Mr Trend, co-owner of the security firm Odegard-Trend. Learning that his partner intends to betray him, Mr Trend hires two professional Exterminators, Crush and Coddish, to terminate Odegard. Crush and Coddish kill Odegard with bolts of animated lightning from a portable electric generator. The murder has been witnessed by Mrs Trend. Her hubby, trying to cover up his evil plan, goes down to investigate and is fried. The two incompetent Exterminators are then on a hunt for all witnesses. Which leads them to the apartment block where Ajax has been working. The two plots converge, when Nancy – Vic's would-be girlfriend – arrives and is kidnapped by the Exterminators. This leads to the film's lengthy climatic car chase...

Commentary: *Crimewave* was written by the Coens and directed by Joel's ex-boss, Sam Raimi, director of *The Evil Dead* (1983) and latterly *Spiderman* (2002). But what started out as a zany comic book film about serial killers, turned into a nightmare. Citing studio interference, which extended to totally recasting the film a week before shooting, both the Coens and Raimi now disown it.

Well, the film may not be quite as they anticipated but what remains is, among other things, the first indication of the Brothers' ongoing love of The Three Stooges. *Crimewave* is a madcap cartoon of a film.

There is a disorienting clash of periods here – the acting is pure 1950s exploitation, the stunts are lifted from the Keystone Kops silents of the 1920s, the cars seem to be vintage 1970s, the costumes are strictly 1940s, the music revolves around refrains which are distinctly 1930s, yet Vic opens his recollections with the installation of a 1980s video surveillance system. This is just the Coens' way of saying 'Once upon a time...'

The combination of cliché, pastiche and comic-book effects create a film which, rather like its mish-mash of period references, doesn't quite work. The film did not satisfy either Raimi's or the Coens' creative vision for it and the studio interference failed to make it a hit. The Coens learned an important lesson from this film: maintain complete creative control. To this day they write, produce, direct and edit their films and repeatedly hire cast and crew members they know they can trust. Maybe the relative disaster of

Crimewave was a necessary evil, not an intolerable cruelty.

Crimewave's main attraction is the way it served as a dress rehearsal for many of the themes and stylistic conceits which would be given more dignified airings in the Coens' later, more sophisticated, films. Here are a few:

Premonitions: Helene Trend appeared, however obliquely, in *Blood Simple*, as a voice on Meurice's answer-phone. She was voiced by Frances McDormand's then unknown room-mate, Holly Hunter.

The story begins in the Hudsucker State Penitentiary, not greatly dissimilar to that which opens *Raising Arizona*.

The monstrous Exterminators lay the foundations for evil Laurel and Hardy-type double acts in later films: Gale and Evelle in *Raising Arizona* and Walter and Gaear in *Fargo*.

Foreshadowing Charlie Meadows in *Barton Fink*, Crush Exterminator responds badly to being called 'a maniac.'

Regarding the shot where the camera zooms into Mrs Trend's mouth and emerges from the horn of a trumpet, the first half of this was described in the script of *The Hudsucker Proxy*, but not fully used. However, the shot appears in reverse in *Barton Fink*, when it goes into the horn of a trumpet and emerges in the corridor at the Hotel Earle.

The transition to Ajax's story comes in the form of watery flashbacks, like those implemented in *The Hudsucker Proxy*.

As Vic pursues the dame, he winds up with a bucket on his foot like Norville in *The Hudsucker Proxy*.

As the moment of execution draws near, all eyes are drawn to the second hand, drawing inexorably towards the 12, just like the climax of *The Hudsucker Proxy*.

The concierge plunges to his death in a barely competent 'special' effect which is a clear forerunner of the longer, more elaborate, far more expensive Waring Hudsucker plunge.

The idea of a businessman hiring killers who dispose of

his wife deliberately or otherwise has resonance in *Blood Simple* as well as *Fargo*.

Albert, feeding a corpse into a Salvation Army dumpster, is reminiscent of Gaer feeding his 'funny looking' partner into a wood chipper in *Fargo*.

As he is strapped to the electric chair in the film's opening moments, Ajax begins his story. Ed Crane ends his story in the chair in *The Man Who Wasn't There*.

Raising Arizona (1986)
'Sometimes it's a hard world for the little things.'

Cast: Nicolas Cage (Hi), Holly Hunter[2] (Ed), Trey Wilson (Nathan Arizona Snr.), John Goodman[1] (Gale), William Forsythe (Evelle), Sam McMurray (Glen), Frances McDormand[3] (Dot), Randall 'Tex' Cobb (Leonard Smalls), Lynne Dumin Kitei (Florence Arizona), M Emmet Walsh[2] (Machine Shop Earbender)

Crew: Director: Joel Coen, Producer: Ethan Coen, Writers: Joel & Ethan Coen, Cinematographer: Barry Sonnenfeld[2], Music: Carter Burwell[2], Editor: Michael R Miller, Colour, 94 minutes

Plot: H. I. (Hi) McDunnough marries Edwinna (Ed) with the intent of starting a family. Unfortunately, Ed is as barren as the desert they see through their window. As if to mock them, the big news story that week is of the delivery of The Arizona Quints. Ed decides that they must 'adopt' one of the Arizona children.

Hi and Ed's transition from simplistic trailer trash to aspirational Middle Americans was never fated to be a smooth ride, especially as everyone seems determined to take the child from them – including escaped prisoners Gale and Evelle and, most bizarrely, The Lone Biker of the Apocalypse.

This all comes to a head in a huge, chaotic bank robbery/car chase/shoot-out finale...

Commentary: The Coens' scripts are textbook examples of clarity and economy. Almost uniquely, it is possible to read a Coen script as if it were a novel. They work their screenplays so thoroughly that there is very little evolution between the written word and the acted word. They edit their movies on paper a long time before a reel of film gets anywhere near a camera. Consequently very few editorial changes are needed.

One of the rare exceptions to this occurs in the opening moments of *Raising Arizona*, where Hi, in his voice-over, is discussing how it isn't easy to 'stand up and fly straight... with that sunovabitch Reagan in the White House.' Originally, this introduction included the line, 'I'm not complainin', mind you; just sayin' there ain't no pancake so thin it ain't got two sides.' This echoes Visser's opening comments in *Blood Simple*. It is possible that Hi's line was removed so as not to draw a distracting comparison between these two characters so early in the film's development.

As with *The Big Lebowski*, the opening monologue uses the President to establish a date for the film (Bush and the very early 1990s in the case of *The Big Lebowski*, Reagan and the mid-1980s for *Raising Arizona*) although, just to be perverse, they have included a subtitle which tells you the exact day and time of the kidnapping – but not the year.

Hi is a character almost entirely devoid of character. Although he is generally well meaning, he simply has no backbone. He doesn't want to hurt anyone, which is why he can never bring himself to load the guns he takes on robberies, but then he can rarely bring himself to stand up for himself either. He's a child. He reacts childishly to his situation, browbeaten into accepting the deranged wisdom of Ed because he hasn't the nerve to contradict her.

Gale and Evelle are similarly childish. They are the school yard bullies who feign friendship with Hi whilst it suits them (when they need a hideaway) but turn on him as soon as they find he has something worth money (little Nathan Jnr.). When they are being friendly they endeavour to entangle him in their life of crime and, because he is so susceptible to suggestion, he is tempted. Until Ed changes his mind back for him.

In this respect, Hi fits neatly alongside Ray from *Blood Simple*, the eponymous Barton Fink, *The Hudsucker Proxy*'s Norville Barnes, *Fargo*'s Jerry Lundegaard, The Dude in *The Big Lebowski* and Miles Massey in *Intolerable Cruelty* as the nice but dim character who gets swept along in incidents which are simply beyond him.

Neither Hi nor Ed have the maturity, the social circle or the vocabulary to make their dream of upward mobility a reality. In his internal monologues, there is an amusing grandiloquence to Hi's language, possibly inherited from the Old South where he also gained his accent: '...her insides were a rocky place where my seed could find no purchase...' and '...He left a scorched earth in his wake, befouling even the sweet desert breeze that whipped across his brow...' demonstrate a great pleasure in the exploration of language. But, somewhere between thought and expression, this is lost and he is left uttering things like, 'Better hurry it up. I'm in dutch with the wife.'

The manipulation of language is an important ingredient in a Coen film, they clearly love writing dialogue which avoids getting to any obvious point. For Hi, the fact that he will never be able to elucidate the complex and almost poetic thoughts rolling around in his head is the key to his inevitable failure as a social climber. That and the fact that he is dogged at his every turn by his criminal past.

Having liberated little Nathan Jnr., Hi takes the first

family photo, to immortalise this moment: 'Everything decent and normal from here on out!' Yet it is at this precise moment that their past comes back to haunt them. The flashgun pop becomes a crash of lightning as we cut to the rain-lashed field outside Hi's old prison. Gale bursts out of the mud – a golem, a howling demon belched from the primordial sludge. It is as if the undead were coming back to punish Hi and Ed. This 'birth' is accompanied by Gale's primal scream. This roar, made all the more terrifying by the sheer imposing size of John Goodman, will become something of a signature of his subsequent Coen films.

The feeling that Gale and Evelle Snopes are in some way demonic is reinforced by their reaction to Nathan Jnr.: 'You've been at the Devil's work!' The Snopes boys were born of earth and water. A far more terrifying spectre is born of a curtain of air and fire. The Lone Biker of the Apocalypse is an avenging angel, racing down the long, straight deserted highway, so very similar to the road Ray and Abby travelled in *Blood Simple*. He is 'a man with all the powers of Hell at his command... He was especially hard on the little things... the helpless and the gentle creatures.' Although he would never recognise it in himself, Hi is himself somewhat helpless and relatively gentle.

Nature rumbles and roars here in the form of rain and fire and Gale (named after a howling wind) – much as machines rumbled threateningly throughout *Blood Simple*. Hi feels the ominous approach of thunder. Then there is the even more disturbing rumble from the sun, all of which is drawn together in the roar of The Biker's engine and the fire he leaves in his wake.

As The Biker roars along, he sets a desert flower on fire – this symbolises Ed to Hi (his opening chat-up line was to compare Ed to a desert flower) and shows how threatened he feels. This black-clad creature also represents Hi's not-too-deeply buried guilt. '...He was The Fury That Would Be as soon as Florence Arizona found her little Nathan gone.' This sort of deep-seated trauma clearly tortures him every time he commits a crime, which may explain why he was initially so positive about prison life – it took away the temptation and the resulting pain.

It is the nature of the Coen universe for little or nothing to be quite what it appears. The Lone Biker of the Apocalypse proves to be less of a threat to Hi and Ed than the people much closer at hand. Glen returns and threatens Hi with jail unless he hands over the baby. Since Hi's world has become a roaring maelstrom of chaos, this is possibly more appealing than Glen wishes.

When The Biker arrives at Nathan Arizona's kingdom, 'Unpainted Arizona,' the music and quick close-up clips resemble the montages which introduce the anti-heroes of a Leone Western, or of the slow bit-by-bit introduction to the leather-clad hero in *Mad Max* (1979).

Paradoxically, The Biker is very softly spoken and goes by the name Leonard Smalls. Lenny, to his friends. He hunts escaped prisoners... and babies. When Arizona refuses to take the bait, Smalls disappears... in a puff of cigar smoke.

Much later, after the battle has ended, the nemesis has been defeated and order has resumed, Hi and Ed find that their big adventure into parenthood has effectively come to an end. They have returned to sanity and do the decent thing by taking Nathan Jnr. home.

After the visually idiosyncratic sequences which preceded it, this solemn reunion is a scene devoid of stylistic conceit, which presents everyone, finally, as simply being human. Hi, decent until the last, offers himself to Arizona as a sacrifice, his last-ditch attempt to fulfil his husbandly duty in protecting his wife. Arizona sees something of himself in their childlessness and relents. At that moment, the madness has ended. Nathan Snr. has ceased his posturing, Ed is calm and sane, and Hi is relaxed and cogent. Everything is back in its place. Nathan's in his cot and all's well with the world.

Families: Even more than may be immediately apparent, this film is about families. Back in the mid-1980s, Reagan-omics was at its peak. The yuppie products of that system rolled off the white middle-class production line in their braces, fondling their bulging filofaxes and buying the big house, the flash car, the trophy wife – all they needed to complete the picture of success, was the ultimate fashion accessory: a son they could give their name to.

This social trend created a whole generation of broody young men and women whom Hollywood furnished product for. Hence, *Baby Boom* (1987), *Three Men and a Baby* (1987), *Parenthood* (1989) and *Look Who's Talking* (1989) among many others.

Both of the Coens were newly married in the mid-1980s. Both had money in their pocket for the first time. Clearly, they saw the conformity being displayed by their acquisitive peers and determined to satirise it.

On the most obvious level, the plot revolves around Ed's desperate need to be a mother, which is mirrored in Nathan and Florence Arizona's own fruitless marriage. The difference is that the Arizonas can afford fertility treatment and Ed and Hi cannot.

Ed marries Hi without knowing the first thing about him, simply because he asks and she needs a man to help her become a mother. Her whole personality revolves around this single objective. As an ex-police officer, her morality is entirely switched off when she and Hi hatch the idea of 'adopting' Nathan Jnr.

When Hi holds up a drugstore for a packet of Huggies, Ed, incensed that he should be offering such a bad example

35

to their son, drives off and leaves him, screaming 'You son of a bitch' as she disappears into the night.

Later, when little Nathan has been taken from them, she sits catatonic because her personality has shut down without her borrowed baby. However, finally, she can identify with Florence Arizona, and realises just what she has done and who she has become. Does she accept the responsibility for her madness? No. She effectively shifts the blame onto Hi and insinuates that it is his criminal past that has dragged her down to his level: 'If I'm as selfish and irresponsible as you – if I'm as bad as you, what good're we to each other?'

Hi also has a need, to leave his recidivist days behind him and go forward into 'a brighter future.' In other words, he wants the 'American Dream.' This too is reflected in Nathan Arizona's life, given that he is a self-made millionaire with a shadier past than he would like to admit.

The dark side of successful parenting, if you will, is represented by Dot and Glen and their tribe of monstrous children. They seem to be a warning about being careful what you wish for – you might just have to put it through college. Dot shows that the transformative power of the need to mother is not merely Ed's affliction: '...she wants something to cuddle.' If that means stealing a child already stolen, so be it. Easy come, easy go.

The father figures in the film are presented in no more of a flattering light than the mothers. Nathan Snr. can't tell his children apart. Glen proudly announces that 'there's something wrong with m'semen,' indicating that his children are nothing more to him than tokens of his lost virility. And no matter how well meaning Hi may be, the guy clearly hasn't a clue. When he kidnaps the little'un, he also steals a copy of *Dr Spock's Baby and Child Care* but it remains unread throughout the film.

When Gale and Evelle counter-kidnap Nathan Jnr., they

too take the book and fail to learn anything from it. From the very first, Gale refers to the child as 'a little outlaw,' so he obviously feels an affinity for the boy. This is thrown into sharp relief when the brothers leave Nathan in the middle of the road (the first time). Their reaction is a hysterical primal scream of realisation, as they feel a part of their family has been torn from them. When they retrieve him, he has ceased to be a drooling poker chip ready for cashing – they have learned to value him. 'Promise we ain't never gonna give him up, Gale!' begs Evelle. He is promptly reassured: 'He's our little Gale Jnr., now!' So they are now not merely brothers, they are fathers to the same child. Did one so young ever have so much paternity?

Gale and Evelle are brothers and, in case I haven't mentioned it yet, Joel and Ethan Coen are brothers, so their perception of brotherhood will be based on a lifetime's research. Hi opens the film by mentioning the 'spirit of camaraderie,' or brotherhood, felt in the joint. Nathan the quint, obviously, has a fair few brothers of his own. Then there is the small matter of Lenny, The Lone Biker of the Apocalypse. Although there is no mention of it in the script, Lenny and Hi have something in common – a Woody Woodpecker tattoo. This, combined with Lenny's confession '...when I was a lad, I m'self fetched $30,000 on the black market...', would seem to suggest that he and Hi are, in fact, long-lost brothers.

The *absence* of family is also a theme here. In prison, Gale's opening line is 'Sometimes career gotta come before family!' Yet, he later advises Ed, 'Ya don't breastfeed him, he'll hate you for it later. That's why we wound up in prison... Anyway, that's what Dr Schwartz tells us.' This indicates the pop-psychology notion that the lack of a good family will drive a child to crime. This has obviously come from their prison therapy sessions and they use it as a convenient excuse, but it allows for Lenny Smalls' career as a bounty hunter to be explained by his 'Mama Didn't Love Me' tattoo.

Dreams: There are two lines of reasoning to explain why Lenny Smalls first appears bursting through a wall of fire into Hi's guilty dream. Firstly, he could be simply a figment of Hi's subconscious, of the imagination he fails to display when awake. Secondly, and far more interestingly, there is the prospect that Hi's dreams can predict what is going to happen, or even actually make things happen.

This opens up the third possibility that, since the opening monologue makes it clear that we are seeing this film from Hi's perspective, maybe he is elaborating a little in the retelling. Maybe The Biker was less like the stylised villain of a spaghetti western. Maybe Gale and Evelle were less single-minded. Maybe Hi and Ed didn't kidnap a baby after all. Maybe they just thought about it!

So, if we are to accept the possibility that Hi's slumbering mind may be capable of more than most, the dream in which he wallows during the film's closing moments, changes from one of self-delusion to one of self-fulfilment: Two people who bear a striking resemblance to Hi and Ed (though changed by time) live to a ripe old age and see their family grow and flourish. Hi, of course, has doubts: '…was I wishful thinking? Was I just fleein' reality, like I know I'm liable to do?' Well, possibly for the first time in the whole movie, he's not deluding himself, he's simply developing a realistic ambition. All of which rounds off the tale in a satisfyingly circular way – as the beginning fast-forwards into the present, so the end fast-forwards into the future.

Miller's Crossing (1989)
'Look in your heart.'

Cast: Gabriel Byrne (Tom), Marcia Gay Harden[1] (Verna), John Turturro[1] (Bernie), Albert Finney (Leo), Jon Polito[1] (Johnny), J. E. Freeman (Eddie), Mike Starr (Frankie), Steve Buscemi[1] (Mink), Frances McDormand[4] (Mayor's Secretary), Sam Raimi[2] (Snickering Gunman), Michael Badalucco[1] (Caspar's Driver)

Crew: Director: Joel Coen, Producer: Ethan Coen, Writers: Joel & Ethan Coen, Cinematographer: Barry Sonnenfeld[3], Music: Carter Burwell[3], Editor: Roderick Jaynes[2], Colour, 116 minutes

Plot: An unnamed Eastern Town in the 1920s is run by Irish gang boss Leo O'Bannion. His adviser is Tom Regan. Bookmaker Bernie Bernbaum is gypping Leo out of money by fiddling the odds on boxing matches. Problem is, Leo is in love with Bernie's sister, Verna.

Rival Italian mobster Johnny Caspar sees Leo getting a bit long in the tooth for such a position of authority. Consequently, war breaks out between their gangs. Leo and Tom fall out, so Tom offers his services to Caspar. As a loyalty test, Tom is asked to execute Bernie. Where do Tom's loyalties really lie and who will be the last man standing when the suspicion and betrayal lead to its inevitably violent conclusion?

Commentary: *Miller's Crossing* is either a self-indulgent look at the gangster genre, unsure whether it is an homage or a parody, or a highly stylised, pithy film that plays with the conventions of the gangster film and comes out a winner.

Unlike *Blood Simple* and *Raising Arizona*, where the camera is constantly on the move, the camera often remains motionless here. When it does move, it slowly circles seated characters. This calm, deliberate use of the camera corresponds with Tom's dour acceptance of his fate and his inability to panic no matter how much of a threat he is facing.

As with any good period piece, the production and costume design are exhaustively researched, so even those who can't follow the plot can marvel at the cut of the suits. Certainly a beautiful film to look at and listen to, it is unfortunately lacking in heart, much as Tom is rumoured to be.

Like *Blood Simple*, the film's passion is for the violence, not the romance. The love scenes we see between Tom and Verna are cold and emotionless business arrangements: Verna wants Tom to help her brother. Tom wants to turn Leo against her. Genuine tenderness and understanding exists only between Tom and Leo.

The Brothers Coen have often referred to *Miller's Crossing* as their Dashiell Hammett film. Certainly, one can find two Hammett stories lurking in the text: *Red Harvest* and *The Glass Key*. Indeed, the similarities are so pronounced, that John Harkness remarked, in his *Sight and Sound* review, that he was surprised the Hammett estate didn't sue for plagiarism. *Red Harvest* has had many cinematic reworkings: it was the basis of Kurosawa's *Yojimbo* (1961), Leone's *A Fistful of Dollars* (1964) and Walter Hill's *Last Man Standing* (1997). All of these concern a lone character who enters town and plays its two gangs off against each other. *The Glass Key* is virgin territory by comparison, having only been filmed twice, with

George Raft in 1935 and Alan Ladd in 1942. This is the story of a politician's aide who appears to turn against his boss, but is actually playing both sides in order to help his boss.

Although the Coens credit Hammett as their direct inspiration, the film and characters also reflect the work of Raymond Chandler, whose definition of the hard-boiled hero could have been written for Tom: 'Down these mean streets a man must go who is not himself mean, who is neither tarnished nor afraid... a man of honour, by instinct, by inevitability, without thought of it, and certainly without saying it.' Like Chandler's stories, *Miller's Crossing* is gloomy, downbeat and inadequately plotted. What makes Chandler, Hammett and, for that matter, the Coens a cut above the rest is their skill at weaving vivid, evocative prose, heavy with user-friendly metaphors and similes. They use clever dialogue which epitomises the time and place in which it was written.

In keeping with its inspirations, *Miller's Crossing* opens with a monologue, a familiar device to Coen viewers but, unusually, this is an on-screen monologue delivered by Johnny Caspar. He is this film's streetwise philosopher (another Coen staple) and the subject on which he is holding forth is the importance of ethics in professional gangsterism. In this respect he is a gangster of the old school, despite being a Johnny-come-lately to this particular crime scene.

This opening duplicates that of *The Godfather* (1971), with a close-up of a gangster asking his boss for a favour. Even the lighting and the wooden Venetian blind in the background serve to remind one of that 'I love America' moment.

In common with *Blood Simple* and *Raising Arizona*, the plot here pivots on a fulcrum of confusion and non-communication. What is different from those earlier films is that the viewer is also kept in the dark. This is due to the absence of internal monologue.

Miller's Crossing is Tom's film. People say that Tom is a

thinker not a talker. He certainly doesn't talk to the audience and therefore remains an enigma. Several times people make him offers, to which he replies, 'I'll think about it.' We have to judge what is going on, and why, from what little we see and hear, we never get to find out what he is thinking. 'You always know why you do things?' he asks Leo at one point. This is a key question in a Coen movie. Leo answers, 'Yeah,' and given that he is at heart a simple man, he's probably telling the truth. Nothing is that clear cut for Tom.

Tom is a solitary and tough man. He is the man behind the man who, through his travels, meets dark and eccentric characters. He is judged by the language he uses or, more properly, by his silences; very little is given away about the man. He hides behind irony, the wisecracks and the violence but inside he is a lonely and bitter man known for his heavy drinking, his hopeless gambling and a passion for fashion.

Miller's Crossing is very much a sitting-down film. Its innumerable conversations are carried out in large, opulent offices, warehouses, apartments or speakeasies – all huge, empty locations which emphasise the space between the characters. The only time these men stand up is to knock somebody else down. Usually Tom.

When Tom is first beaten – by Verna in the women's room – his wounded male pride insists that he is capable of 'raising Hell!' Although that only slowly and incrementally happens in the pejorative sense, this wouldn't be a Coen film without a little literal Hell. This is first glimpsed in Leo's house during his attempted murder, which culminates in his house being turned into a raging, bloodstained inferno. It begins quietly with the sound of a brief off-screen struggle. Leo's bodyguard lies prone across his newspaper, his cigarette burning a hole in the page. Upstairs, a wind-up gramophone scratches out the emotive strains of 'Danny Boy' as Leo, wrapped in silk pyjamas and a robe, relaxes alone in bed and enjoys a cigar.

He smells something and then notices a wisp of smoke creep through between the floorboards. Stepping out of bed, he takes the trouble to slip on his velvet slippers, before diving under the bed and shooting the ankles out from under his attackers. Appropriating a dead thug's machine-gun, Leo walks slowly (there being no other way of doing anything in this movie) down the centre of the road, away from the burning shell of his house, shooting the getaway car, until he forces it off the road and into a tree. The burning car reminds Leo of his half-smoked cigar, which he removes from his pocket and continues to smoke.

This scene of fire and brimstone and extreme physical violence shows that, although he may be outwardly misguided and weak now, Leo is as tough as nails underneath. Far tougher, in fact, than Tom. Leo is later described as 'an artist with a Thompson' and for the first time you get an inkling of how he came to be boss. Later, by contrast, when Tom tries to be physically heroic, by running to head off Bernie, it backfires and he gets another of his regular kickings. He is not good at action. He's a plotter and a planner, not a doer. Indeed, he is so passive, he learns to accept the inevitability of his constant beatings.

The film's turning point is when Tom tells Leo that he and Verna were together. Tom then turns his back on his friend and leaves. Leo appears behind him, rolling up his sleeves, all heads turn as Leo passes, eagerly waiting to see Tom get another beating. As Tom skids to a halt at the bottom of the stairs, we can hear the strains of 'Goodnight Sweetheart,' significant if you are following the film's homosexual subtext. Homosexual subtext? Don't panic, all will become clear shortly.

From the moment he throws Tom out to the drama's epilogue, Leo disappears from the narrative. Tom has to spend time in exile to bring about a lasting peace. Although Tom and Leo have fallen out, Tom and Verna soon get it together again. During a post-coital discussion of his break-up with Leo, Verna sarcastically remarks that Tom is 'all heart.' Little does she know.

The next reference to hearts comes from her brother Bernie, in the film's other great moment – the first visit to the woods at Miller's Crossing. Although this is the first time any of the characters have visited this site before, Tom and we, the viewer, have seen it before as the background for Tom's floating-hat dream.

Having now left the 'potato eaters,' Tom is working for the 'eye-ties' and has been tasked to take Bernie out into the wilderness and 'put one in the brain.' Out amongst the trees, these soldiers are on unfamiliar turf. It must seem to Tom that the carpet of dead leaves is emblematic of Leo's fading grip on the town. He has come to the end of his season.

Bernie, talking fast and furious, begs Tom to 'Look in your heart...' and falls to his knees. Finally, reminded of Verna's love for her brother and his own unwillingness to cross a moral line, he makes the decision to let Bernie go. This is the first decision he makes motivated by compassion for Verna – all the others are motivated by compassion for Leo. This shift in loyalty will prove to be a mistake because Bernie is too arrogant to accept the gift Tom has offered him.

Tom is now caught in the middle. He's not trusted by his ex-boss or his current boss. Bernie comes back to haunt him and Verna, believing Tom killed Bernie, now hates him. It's all very *Blood Simple*-ish. Most importantly, the Dane begins to wonder if Bernie really is dead, so goes back to Miller's Crossing to check.

Once again, Tom finds himself walking through the pale, beautiful trees where haunting Oirish music whistles through the leaves. Incongruously, one of his companions, Frankie the thug, feels inspired to air his astonishingly beautiful singing voice. The rules really are different out here.

Tom believes these tall, almost unnaturally straight boughs are going to be the last thing he sees before he dies. The Dane wants to see Bernie's corpse or else 'we leave a fresh one.' Just as the Dane is levelling his gun on Tom's head, a body dressed in Bernie's clothes is found. Tom is saved... for today.

In contrast to all the other characters in the film, for whom the consequences of violence are serious, when Tom gets beaten up, he gets nothing worse than a split lip. Eight times he is beaten up and each time his wounds are gone by the next morning, ready for the next beating.

Nevertheless, his powers of persuasion soon return after his weakness at Miller's Crossing, and he begins to plant seeds of doubt in Caspar's simple mind, that the Dane is double-crossing him. As Caspar makes his decision about whether he believes the Dane or Tom – the Coen keynote rumblings begin in the background – the fire behind Caspar roars its encouragement. The photography becomes stylised for the first time in the film and, to the accompaniment of a howling fat man (sitting in for the various John Goodman roles), Caspar decides. As he brings the fire iron down on the Dane's head again and again, he is sprayed with blood and thunder rolls overhead, as if Heaven itself were being torn apart. Tom really is raising Hell. He looks on in dazed horror at what his scheming has wrought.

This scene of Biblical horror and the confession scene between Tom and Verna, immediately after it, which is played out in the rain-soaked Chinatown district, both evoke the early violence-soaked moments of *Once Upon a Time in America* (1983).

That night at the Barton Arms (Tom's apartment block) the strands of Tom's web finally converge, as Bernie and Caspar are drawn fatally together. As Caspar's corpse lies cooling on the landing, this time his face splattered with his own blood, Tom convinces Bernie to hand over his gun and pin Caspar's murder on the Dane.

As he speaks, Tom is preparing to cross a line he has never previously crossed. To accompany this, an ominous rumble once again fills the background. Then Tom turns the gun on Bernie. Tom has taken Bernie's betrayal personally. This is the first time Tom has levelled his gun in anger during the film. Bernie has changed him. When he once more begs, 'Look in your heart...' Tom's response is simple, emphatic and honest, 'What heart?' He has become the living embodiment of his own pessimistic theory, 'Nobody knows anybody, not that well.' Not well enough to know if they're capable of killing. No one believes he is, which is why his plan ultimately works. But, sufficiently motivated, anyone is capable of plumbing any depth.

The film's final scene returns to the rural idyll where it began. It is Bernie's funeral and only Leo, Verna and Tom are present. Verna won't speak to Tom but Leo begs for Tom to return to the fold. However, although Leo is now safe, he is only safe to marry Verna, and Tom couldn't put up with seeing them together every day. Neither, for that matter, would Verna be able to tolerate seeing the man who murdered her brother.

Although things have outwardly turned full circle, with the status quo reasserted and Leo once more in pole position, the characters have changed. As Leo walks away, alone through an avenue of trees (à la the closing moments of Carol Reed's 1949 film *The Third Man*), Tom watches him go, his face betraying his heartbreak. Finally, we realise that the object of his love is not Verna, but Leo.

References to Tom's heart are littered throughout the film. He is mostly accused of not having one. Yet, throughout, he has been motivated purely by his heart. Tom has risked his reputation, his position and his life for the man he loves. Now, having successfully rebuilt the world in Leo's image, he sacrifices that love in order to give Leo and Verna's marriage its greatest chance of survival. Tom steps aside.

In the film's closing frames the audience get to look in Tom's heart, to see the face of his unrequited love and to understand the true nature of his heroism. Like the hat in his dream, Tom is prepared to let Leo just blow away.

Families: Tom is seeing Verna, who is officially Leo's girl. This is an Oedipal-type incestuous relationship because the head of the organisation is usually the father figure (especially if the organisation calls itself The Family) and Leo calls Tom 'kid.' If Verna is the symbolic mother, this makes Tom and Verna's relationship tantamount to incest.

However, this film seems anti-Oedipal because Leo is far from the masterful head of this particular family. Apart from when wielding a tommy-gun, he is actually weak and confused by his relationship with Verna. He is a passive character, largely at the mercy of Tom's whim.

By protecting the woman he loves, Leo begins a war. He refuses to admit that his time is past and insists he can '...still swap body blows with any man in this city... except you, Tom.' 'Or Verna!' adds Tom. He has been emasculated by his relationship. Tom, who doesn't love women, doesn't suffer such weakness. He is steely-eyed clear at all times.

Bernie claims that his sister has taught him something about 'the bedroom arts,' which introduces genuine incest into this family. Bernie is also in a homosexual relationship with Mink (Steve Buscemi) – not for emotional needs, but as a business decision. As fight fixers for the respective gangs, they represent a marriage of business interests.

So we already have a dysfunctional family riven by incest and overtones of homosexuality. This seems as good a time as any to justify the claim that Tom and Leo are actually in love with each other... Look at the way Leo never considers that Verna might be staying with Tom and how he reacts when he finds out she was. When he throws Tom out, he calls it 'the kiss-off.' Examine the film's last shot, the look of barely restrained pain on Tom's face as Leo walks away into marriage. Although Leo doesn't realise any of this consciously, Tom is too intelligent not to.

This undercurrent is an established ingredient in gangster movies. In *Little Caesar* (1930), Rico (Edward G Robinson) had a homosexual love for Mascara (Douglas Fairbanks Jnr.). In *Scarface* (1932 and 1983) Paul Muni and Al Pacino had a fatal incestuous love for their sister. And in *White Heat* (1949), Cody Jarrett (Jimmy Cagney) had an incestuous love for his mother. Therefore, *Miller's Crossing* is about a war that is averted because of an undeclared homosexual attraction.

Dreams: Where *Raising Arizona* ends with the main character's dream, *Miller's Crossing* begins with one. We see a hat swooping sedately through the leaf clutter of an idyllic countryside scene. Did we but know it at the time, this is as much of an insight into the workings of Tom Regan's mind as we're going to get.

Sometime later, Tom tells Verna about his dream of the hat blowing away. Verna tries to complete his dream, 'You chased the hat, and it changed into something else.' But she's wrong. He doesn't chase it – he just lets it blow away. 'No, it's just a hat! There's nothing more foolish than a man chasing his hat.' Yet we first meet her when he goes to her apartment, chasing his hat.

Barton Fink (1991)
'I'll show you the life of the mind!'

Cast: John Turturro[2] (Barton Fink), John Goodman[2] (Charlie Meadows), Judy Davis (Audrey Taylor), Michael Lerner (Jack Lipnick), John Mahoney[1] (W. P. Mayhew), Tony Shalhoub[1] (Ben Geyser), Jon Polito[2] (Lou Breeze), Steve Buscemi[2] (Chet)

Crew: Director: Joel Coen, Producer: Ethan Coen, Writers: Joel & Ethan Coen, Cinematographer: Roger Deakins[1], Music: Carter Burwell[4], Editor: Roderick Jaynes[3], Colour, 116 minutes

Plot: It is 1941. Barton Fink, a playwright snapped up by Hollywood, finds himself booking into the ominous Hotel Earle. When he settles down to write, noises from next door start to disturb him. When he complains, his neighbour – a hulking insurance salesman called Charlie Meadows – stomps round and, much to Barton's surprise, they hit it off.

After Charlie leaves, Barton finds that he can't write. The ideas won't flow. To find inspiration, he approaches celebrated novelist W P Mayhew. Unfortunately, Mayhew is consumed by his own inner demons. Mayhew's 'secretary,' Audrey is more helpful, especially in unleashing Barton's tightly restrained libido.

The next morning, Barton wakes to find Audrey dead

beside him. Charlie comes to save the day, then leaves Barton to look after a mysterious box.

Barton soon learns that Charlie is actually Karl 'Madman' Mundt, who decapitates his victims. Barton looks suspiciously at the box. It's about head size. Realisation begins to dawn but instead of horror, Barton finds inspiration...

Commentary: *Barton Fink* is the most personal expression yet made by the Brothers Coen. It deals with the power wielded by writers. It was inspired by a writer's block they claim to have suffered whilst struggling to make sense of *Miller's Crossing.* Pragmatically, they decided to leave *Miller's Crossing* alone for a while and wrote a script about writer's block instead. The fact that their titular character is a Jewish writer with Joel's thick wiry hair and Ethan's small round spectacles is, of course, purely coincidental.

The film begins as it ends, with wallpaper. Old, faded paper, with a shrub design repeated across it. Why wallpaper? Well, of course, what wallpaper does particularly well is cover things up. The question we are being invited to ask from the very first frame of this film is: what lurks behind that innocuous, faintly greenish surface?

Then we are behind the scenes of a New York theatre, standing alongside Barton, the nervous first-time writer. All around him we can see what the theatre audience never sees – the mechanisms at work behind the proscenium arch.

The first lines of dialogue are uttered off screen. Sound is a crucially important storytelling device in this film, and the Coens begin as they mean to go on. The man declares, 'I'm kissing it all goodbye, these four stinking walls, the six flights up, the El train that roars by at 3am like a cast-iron wind.'

These words serve as our introduction to the film as Barton, like Tom Regan, has no internal monologue. You would think a writer would have no problem with elucidating his thoughts and feelings but, as we progressively learn, Barton has very few thoughts and feelings to call his own. He lives purely in a world of 'art.' In essence, he has nothing to say and, as the Coens' most loquacious character yet, wastes no opportunity to say it. Much later, he is told by Audrey, 'Empathy requires understanding!' He, of course, has neither.

Barton is credited with finding 'nobility in the most squalid corners and poetry in the most callused speech.' When pressed about his art, he lapses into well-rehearsed dogma. He insists that he wants to create 'a new living theatre of and about and for the Common Man.' Yet he has no real idea what this Common Man actually is, just a romanticised notion he feels a patronising pity for. And pity is the basest coin there is.

Barton's pragmatic agent tells him to go to Hollywood. 'The Common Man will still be here when you get back.' His reaction is typically deluded, 'It doesn't seem to me that Los Angeles is the place to lead the life of the mind.' The life of his mind is far more important to him than the lives of his fellow human beings.

Of course, if he really wanted to craft social realism out of his art to make some kind of difference, he could do few things less effective than writing a play they will never have the cash or the inclination to see. By contrast, movies present the golden opportunity to make some small difference to the miserable life of the Common Man, by taking his mind off that life for a few hours. If, on the other hand, he doesn't want to make any difference, then he is a parasite, sucking the lifeblood from those less fortunate or less literate than himself.

Barton's arrival in LA is prefigured by a Coen trademark – the mounting off-screen roar. This is the sound of the sparkling blue ocean crashing against a rock. This introductory image of LA is the one that Barton will be left with – a wave of reality and compromise crashing against his immovable self-regard, and slowly eroding it.

The echo of that crashing wave forms the atmosphere inside the Hotel Earle. He presses the bell for attention and the ring echoes on forever. Chet, the omnipresent, omni helpful clerk, emerges cheerfully from a hatch in the floor – obviously he has been called up from a lower level to silence the bell.

Barton is given a room on the sixth floor (as was the character in his play). In the elevator, this number has to be repeated three times. So, before he has even reached his room, the clues are beginning to be assembled about the true nature of the lodgings he has selected.

The corridor to his room is virtually endless and lined with identical doorways, insinuating that the tale we are about to witness could take place in any of these rooms, with any of the hotel's patrons. Wind moans perpetually down this corridor but it seems to be sucking rather than blowing – so the doors wheeze when they are open and are sucked closed again.

Waiting to greet him in his sparse little room, a pad of writing paper declaims the Hotel Earle's motto 'A Day or a Lifetime.' Judging from the layer of dust on it, time has stood still here for a long while. Also, this long-unused sheet of paper, with the unused pencil on it, is portentous of his upcoming writer's block.

Once he has settled in his room, Barton notices the one and only decoration – a picture of a woman sitting on a beach, gazing out to sea. As he regards the vast potential offered by that distant horizon, his ears are filled with the sound of those waves crashing against his rock. Laying down, he gazes up at the paint peeling from the ceiling and hears the faint buzz of something alive in there with him – he assumes it is a mosquito. There is also the muffled sound of someone in the next room, laughing or maybe sobbing.

This is a very still film, largely set in this one small room, yet the work that has gone into layering the sound gives it depth and vibrancy. It is filled with action-packed silences. What we hear, or think we hear, is at least as important as what we see. As he listens to the various curious sounds of the Hotel Earle, Barton drifts off to sleep.

Cut to Link's office. Link is not accustomed to listening. He uses language as a siege weapon, finishing Barton's sentences, bombarding him with unnecessary information, machine-gunning him with undeserved compliments and unsupportable assurances. Here, the Coens are dealing with all of their misgivings about the established Hollywood system into which they have, thankfully, never fitted.

'They tell me you know the poetry of the streets, so this would rule out Westerns, Pirate Pictures, Screwball, Bible, Roman...' Although he insists that he trusts 'That Barton Fink Feeling,' he still proceeds to outline the story Barton must write, without ever once admitting that it is a formula any reasonably well-trained chimp could reproduce.

Everything that he insists is true isn't. All the things that he says are important aren't. This is a use of language which someone as naïve and literal as Barton cannot keep up with. Yet the precise use of language is very important in this film – the Coens' wordiest to date – but the barrage of dialogue doesn't necessarily communicate any better than the extended silences in his hotel room or throughout *Blood Simple*.

Back to the Earle, where non-verbal sound is all-important. As the camera lingers in that long, empty corridor, we hear Barton's typing before we see it, and the first word we see him type is 'audible.' He is bravely plodding on with his Wallace Beery picture, beginning with the only fictional world he knows – that of his notional tenement building and his distant fishmongers. Even in his screenplay, the real world is something that you can only hear at a safe distance.

As he considers the few words he has written, possibly realising just how similar they are to his play, *Bare Ruined Choirs*, he becomes disturbed by those sounds emanating once more through the wall from next door. He's not sure if he can hear laughter or sobbing, but he takes what could very well be the bait, and calls down to Chet to complain.

So it comes to pass that an outside world Barton has never guessed at hammers on the door. Hand pressed painfully to forehead, there stands the intimidating large form of Charlie Meadows, a name which evokes grassy images, like the wallpaper. What secrets could that name be covering up?

Charlie says he sells insurance, 'peace of mind,' yet he has dice on his braces – the symbol of chaos and doubt. In common with all successful insurers, he sells peace of mind by first sowing doubt and fear, 'Fire, theft and casualty are not things that happen to other people.' Not when he's around, they don't.

Barton, as full of his own genius as ever, responds by patronising Charlie: '[I write about] people like you, the average working stiff, the Common Man.' The response is portentous: 'Well, ain't that a kick in the head.' Barton, of course, doesn't notice that this cliché could also be indicative of Charlie's hurt feelings because he is unaware that the Common Man even has normal human feelings.

One thing you can't afford to do when engaged in a verbal power struggle is pay too much attention to the opposition. Consequently, Barton doesn't notice that Charlie's language is also very precise, repeating 'Hell' and 'damn' in almost every speech: 'I feel like Hell'; 'Hell, why not'; 'Damned interesting work'; 'Damned difficult.' Subtle warnings which Barton, of course, misses and will later pay dearly for.

Meanwhile, Barton is continuing to lecture Charlie mercilessly: 'The hopes and dreams of the Common Man are as noble as any King... Don't call it New Theatre, Charlie, call it Our Theatre.' His notions are entirely made of theory, abstracted from any real experience or practice. What Barton is evangelising is what has become known as 'dumping down,' the patronising manner by which the aesthetic elite unilaterally decide what is good for everyone else. After insisting that he and Charlie are of the same stock, bonded together in brotherhood, Barton proceeds to remind Charlie of their separateness: 'To put it in *your* language: the theatre becomes as phoney as a $3 bill!' But isn't that what the theatre is anyway? Phoney constructs of illusion and technique designed to fool and engage the willing audience.

During their first conversation, Barton reassures Charlie that he's 'a real man!' After all, he should know, what with his being the poet of the streets and all. But is that all Charlie is? Beneath the surface of this particular Common Man, a furnace rages, raising the heat in the room and pouring out of him as an unending stream of sweat.

Charlie bids Barton a fond farewell with the confession, 'Too much revelry late at night, you forget there's other people in the world.' This suggests sarcasm because, as he later mentions in passing, he can hear everything that occurs within the Hotel (and possibly further field – much further).

There has been much speculation in the press about this film, as to whether or not the Hotel Earle is Hell, and Charlie the Devil. Well, whilst the evidence would indeed seem to point to Hell (the intolerable heat, the three sixes in the elevator, the fire and brimstone at the end) I'm personally of the opinion that Charlie is not the landlord of this nightmare, but a tenant.

When he breezes in for his second visit, Charlie has a wad of cotton wool stuffed in one ear because of a chronic infection, he needs the wool to 'staunch the flow of pus.' Barton confides in Charlie that he believes his quest in life is to excavate the soul of the working class, and this dredging causes 'the kind of pain most people don't know anything about.' Charlie, on the other hand, knows nothing of the pain suffered by those who don't live in a self-deluded fantasy. Barton fails entirely to acknowledge Charlie's very obvious pain, and its relation to the state of *his* soul.

Although he drinks less than Mayhew, Charlie always has a flask – is he, like Mayhew, building a levee trying to keep all the sounds of the hotel from tormenting him? 'Seems like I hear everything going on in this dump. Pipes, or something.' When the guests in Charlie's hotel suffer, it seems that he suffers with them. It is my contention that he feels the pain of the guests in their own tortured little worlds. Hence the sobbing and the laughing. He's really been living the lives of all the people in his hotel and this is his torture, his punishment, his Hell. Wouldn't that drive you to drink?!

Charlie hardly acts like the Lord of the Underworld. Instead, he seems to be a soul in torment. Maybe he's even a fallen angel, one for whom Hades reserves an especially harsh Damnation – he says at one point that he is 'always on the wing.'

It is not accidental that the goo which drools from his ear is the same colour and consistency as the goo leaking out from behind the wallpaper. The insinuations throughout the film are that the Earle is actually a living entity, with wallpaper for skin and a windswept corridor for a throat, and that Charlie is symbiotically attached to it, like a parasite... or a mosquito.

Referring to the ear infection, Charlie teases the unknowing Barton with 'Well, can't trade my head in for a new one.' 'No,' replies the innocent Bart, 'I guess you're stuck with the one you've got.' Of course, a deeply hidden part of

Charlie's personality actually doesn't seem to agree with this philosophy. Quite the opposite, in fact.

In a scene which was mysteriously cut from the film, but is retained in the script, Charlie leaves his cotton wad in Barton's sink so that it clogs the plughole, symbolising Barton's writer's block, which only settles on him after his first meeting with Charlie. Is it a side effect of his contact with Charlie or a deliberate curse?

'Beery? Wrestling picture? Could be a pip!' Whilst Barton has very probably never heard of Wallace Beery, Charlie is a fan. He loves the mass-produced nonsense which Hollywood churns out to sedate the masses. When he offers to show Barton some wrestling, Barton admits that he isn't 'interested in the act itself.' This is because it's too physical and too real. His ideas are born out of ignorance and wouldn't survive a sudden dose of education. This is why he admires the working stiff whilst demonstrating no knowledge of what it is like to actually work.

The next time Charlie enters, his language has subtly changed. He seems to be concerned now with the concept of Redemption. He says 'Jesus' and 'God' a lot. He talks about people who are cruel to him because of his weight – but that's 'my cross to bear.' And all this while he's trying to offer people 'a little peace of mind.' Of course, he has no peace himself.

Telling his stories may offload some of the pain he has vicariously experienced and hence reduce his suffering. This would give him peace of mind. So simply listening would be the most compassionate thing Barton could do. But, of course, he's too self-obsessed.

'Listen to me bellyaching as if my problems amounted to a hill of beans... [to paraphrase *Casablanca*, a film which won't be released for another year]... how goes the life of the mind?'

In response, Barton inadvertently strikes upon the truth: 'Maybe I only had one idea in me – my play. Maybe when that was done, I was done being a writer.'

Seeing the seeds of humility in Barton for the first time, Charlie promptly offers succour by reintroducing his favourite part of biology: 'You've got a head on your shoulders... where there's a head there's hope.' Charlie's subtle allusions to the trouble with the human head continue when he informs Barton that he has to go to New York because things are 'all balled up at head office.'

And so, Barton is left alone, utterly alone, just himself, his typewriter and the punishment Charlie has inflicted on him – the blockage in his own head office. Whenever he begins to sink into the beach photo, he is reawakened by the sound of the wallpaper peeling. The thin skin that hides the unacceptable facts, the cracks and the corruption, is continuing to peel and reveal.

As producer Ben Geisler bombards Barton with ideas in the studio café, they sit next to a painted vista of New York – another artificial depiction of Barton's home town, just like the one in his writing. Geisler, who constantly throws Barton a lifeline, suggests he talk to another writer – i.e. forget about these 'real' people, talk to another creator.

Enter W P (Bill) Mayhew. He is another prime example of the disparity between outward appearance and inner truth. Outwardly, he is a gracious Southern gentleman. Inwardly, he is a chasm of despair. Twice we hear Mayhew raging at the world, both times in the privacy of his own bungalow. He cries that 'the water's lapping up.' His primal fear is drowning in the compromise and mundanity of Hollywood, much as Barton fears he will be gradually eroded by it.

Barton believes and states that Bill's block is caused by the booze, but the booze is the sedative for the pain the not-writing causes. He and Barton represent the two opposite poles of creativity. Mayhew drinks because he has lost this peace of mind. For him, the grand productive years are gone, and there is no insurance against that.

As Barton reels off one of his polemics about there being no art without pain, the camera holds on Audrey because, we later learn, she is really the creative half of the team. Bill's response is: 'Well, me, I just enjoy making things up... it's when I can't write, can't escape from myself, that I want to rip my head off.' Again, the head.

So Barton writes out of masochism, whereas Mayhew writes to ease the pain. But, of course, neither of these stated positions reveals the full story. When Mayhew refers to his writing, he is really referring to Audrey's. When Barton refers to his, he means his one and only play. Audrey, then, the least melodramatic of the three, is the truly gifted one and, as such, Barton should listen to her advice.

Later, when she comes over to help him with his script, she reveals to him a considerable trade secret, that 'art' is as much about technique as it is inspiration: 'It's really just a formula. You don't have to type your soul into it.' Is this emblematic of the defensive posture the Coens inevitably assume when being questioned about their work, by repeatedly insisting it has no meaning and they just make it up as they go along?

The morning after Audrey's seduction of him, Barton watches the mosquito sucking her blood – as if it isn't interested in him any more. Of course, her blood is in somewhat short supply because it leaked a lot when she was murdered. He screams. Charlie, who must have heard the scream, comes running, almost as if he has been awaiting his cue. Barton is confused and divided. When Charlie initially asks if he is all right, he nods when he says no, but means yes – his head is betraying him.

When Barton finally decides to ask Charlie's help, the big man won't let him into his room (having previously described it as, 'A Helluva mess'). Instead, they go back to Barton's room, as if the secret Charlie has to hide is worse than the one Barton has to reveal.

Barton stands in the bathroom, vulnerable and cold in his underwear, and studies the veins and arteries flexing just beneath the skin of his bare feet. In the bedroom, Charlie can be heard sorting things and saying, 'put this totally out of your head.' In the script, Barton is described as 'shut down... not in control.' He is demonstrating Charlie-like characteristics. It can't be too long before he too starts banging his forehead to dislodge stubborn thoughts.

In the very next scene, Lipnick, the other fat manipulator in Barton's life, in a similar state of undress, similarly instructs Barton to 'put it out of your head,' when he temporarily fires his assistant Lou. This proximity and repetition links Lipnick to Charlie, both in size and inclination. They are the two men who lead the innocent Bart out of his insular little life of the mind.

Back in room 621, Barton gets hysterical: 'I think I'm losing my mind!' He is, or rather, he's having it taken from him. Charlie's response is typically calculated: 'We've gotta keep our heads.' He then follows this by asking Barton to look after his box, which he claims contains everything of value in his life. Not for the first time, he says this must seem pathetic and, not for the first time, Barton's response is motivated by self-pity: 'You've got more than I have!'

Outside, an unseen dog barks like Cerberus, welcoming Barton to Hell. At which moment, he opens the drawer in his desk and happens upon a Bible he hasn't noticed before. If we are to accept the analogy between the Hotel Earle and Hell, then this must surely be an olive branch from Heaven, an attempt at rescue.

Barton being Barton, God of his own deluded little universe, doesn't respond to this. Instead he slumps further into his own rapidly deflating ego and sees his script's opening paragraph as the opening verse of 'Genesis.' This is the most literal example of hubris I think I have ever seen. It can't bode well for Barton's immediate future.

The police add another dose of the outside world. They tell Barton that Charlie is really Karl 'Madman' Mundt, a killer who particularly likes hacking the heads off his victims. What does Barton take away from this conversation? Revulsion? Terror? No, he re-enters his room and regards Charlie's box with renewed fascination. The realisation that it may well contain Audrey's head strangely emboldens him and fires off his creative flow. She was Mayhew's 'golden head,' now she is his.

For the first and only time, as the corridor echoes with his typing, we see one of the other occupants, timidly putting his shoes out for Chet to polish. The damnation of Barton Fink is all but complete. It will soon be time to initiate another supplicant.

Barton finishes his new script and so, liberated from doubt and pain, he gives full rein to the insufferable egotist he carries inside. It is in a dance hall, heaving with servicemen, that we learn of the Japanese attack on Pearl Harbor out in the real world. How much respect does he reserve for these brave, fated, common men? The usual: 'I'm a writer, you monsters. I create! This is how I serve the Common Man!' Yes, they may be going off to die for their country, but that's nothing – he's finished writing a wrestling picture!

After the resulting brawl, he returns to his room to find the police waiting to arrest him for Audrey's murder. Suddenly, he notices the temperature change and realisation dries in his throat: 'It's hot, he's back!' Indeed he is. Charlie

Meadows is no longer divided. There is no more, 'me, myself and I,' there is just Mundt.

Before it is seen, the roar of the fire is heard and its heat felt. The walls are red hot and begin to burn. Mundt steps out of the flames, as Lenny Smalls did. He repeatedly bellows, 'Look upon me. I'll show you the life of the mind!' The flames follow him down the corridor. This is the life of *his* mind. This is the Hell he suffers permanently. The burning, the pain, the chaos, the noise.

Mundt makes short work of the first cop. He breathes, 'Heil Hitler,' into the second cop's petrified face – the anti-Semite who taunted Barton – before blowing it away.

And with that, the rage is over. Mundt is gone, his duty performed, and Charlie has the wheel once more. Disconcertingly calm, he joins Barton for a conversation. When Barton, quite naturally, asks about the 'Madman' appellation, Charlie is philosophical: He points out that he isn't actually mad at people at all. 'Most guys I just feel sorry for! Yeah, it tears me up inside, to think about what they're going through, how trapped they are. I understand it. I feel for them. So I try to help them out... I just wish someone would do as much for me.'

Now, when it's too late, he explains about what it's like when things get all balled up at the head office. 'Sometimes it's so hot, I want to crawl right out of my skin.' Which is what the peeling paper is all about.

Then, after that brief wallow in his own misery, Charlie turns on Barton once more. 'You think you know about pain? You think I've made your life Hell?... You come into my home and complain that I'm making too much noise.' A little human decency, and Barton could have avoided becoming embroiled in this dark fantasy.

Exhausted and disappointed, Charlie returns to his own room. And so Barton's adventure in the Underworld draws to an end. He leaves the Earle, taking his script and Charlie's box ('I lied, it isn't mine!') but, very noticeably, not the one thing he brought with him: his Underwood typewriter. As he walks down the corridor, he is serenaded by one final howling moan. And so the tragic story of Charlie Meadows, a man cursed to inspire then share the pains of the mortal, will continue, but it will do so without Barton Fink.

When Barton emerges once more into what passes for the real world, i.e. Capitol Pictures, he finally learns the true nature of his own punishment: Lipnick hates the script.

He wanted a film about big men in tights: 'Not wrestling with his soul... well maybe just a little for the critics.' This exchange would seem to ring true of the Coens' own experience of film-making – loved by critics, mostly ignored by audiences. Why? Because they have too much soul-searching and not enough wrestling, it seems.

'You think the whole world revolves around whatever rattles around inside that little kike head of yours!' Exactly. And because of that he didn't listen to the instructions Lipnick gave him, nor the advice Geisler provided. (Geisler, too, is out now, because of his association with Barton.) Also, on a more visceral level, this same arrogance has brought about the violent deaths of Barton's only two friends (so, by comparison, Geisler got let off lightly).

And finally, for Barton, a Purgatory of waiting, trapped in the same cage which destroyed Mayhew – the cage of contracted indenture to a tyrant who won't let you practise your art. 'Stay in town!' bellows Lipnick, sealing the door and ensuring that Barton gets to extract the maximum amount of pain from his punishment.

Suddenly, without having seemingly travelled, Barton finds himself on the beach. He sits and watches the water crashing against the rock and the girl from his picture arrives. 'You must be in pictures,' he teases, suddenly adept and unconcerned by the proximity of this siren. 'Don't be silly,' she chides. And that, ultimately, has been Barton's sin. He has been silly. For that he has been dragged through a Hell he barely perceived and is now trapped in a Purgatory made of his own ignorance.

The sight and sound of crashing waves slowly fade out, replaced by that wallpaper, once again hiding that which is best kept secret, protecting the mysterious life of the Brothers Coen's collective mind.

Now comes the question of exactly how much of all this we are to take literally. There are three schools of thought on this matter, so let's deal with them individually:

Firstly, there is the *Brazil* Theory, named after Terry Gilliam's 1985 movie. At the end of that film, Sam Lowry (Jonathan Pryce) goes mad, and therefore escapes into his own fantasy world. So, does Barton's writer's block send him mad, just to get away from the responsibility of having to write another play? Does he, in other words, escape into the life of the mind?

The second hypothesis is known as the *Videodrome* Theory, named after David Cronenberg's 1982 film, wherein Max Renn (James Woods) puts on the Videodrome helmet and, from that moment until the end of the film, his world becomes an hallucinogenic nightmare. The explanation for this is simply that you never see him take the helmet off. The whole second half of the film is a dream. Apply this to *Barton Fink* and you realise that you see Barton drop off to sleep when he arrives at Hotel Earle, but you don't see him wake up, and from then on weird things start to happen.

Then there's the *Apocalypse Now/Buffy the Vampire Slayer* Theory, which simply states that the world really is that weird if you look at it the wrong way. Maybe there really is chaos just round the corner. Maybe a fallen angel really is your neighbour. And maybe powers far beyond our comprehension really are at work just beyond our line of sight. This is a theme we shall return to in *The Hudsucker Proxy*.

Dreams: The opening lines of dialogue in this film are from Barton's play. His female character scorns the ambition of the male character as, 'Dreaming again!' The man retorts, 'I'm awake now, awake for the first time in years. Daylight is a dream if you've lived with your eyes closed.'

So the opening dialogue exchange concerns a sleeper awaking. Given Barton's almost total ignorance of the real life of the Common Man he so adores, it could well be said that he lives with his eyes closed!

The Hudsucker Proxy (1994)
'The future is now.'

Cast: Tim Robbins (Norville Barnes), Jennifer Jason Leigh (Amy Archer), Paul Newman (Sidney Mussburger), John Mahoney[2] (Chief), Charles Durning[1] (Waring Hudsucker), Jim True (Buzz), William Cobbs (Moses), Bruce Campbell[2] (Smitty), Steve Buscemi[3] (Beatnik Barman), Peter Gallagher (Vic Teneta), Sam Raimi[3] (Hudsucker Brainstormer)

Crew: Director: Joel Coen, Producer: Ethan Coen, Writers: Joel & Ethan Coen & Sam Raimi, Cinematographer: Roger Deakins[2], Music: Carter Burwell[5] & Aram Khachaturian, Editor: Thom Noble, Colour, 111 minutes

Plot: Waring Hudsucker throws himself from the 44th floor of the mighty Hudsucker Building (45th if you include the Mezzanine). Sidney Mussburger takes control of the Board and snatches Norville Barnes from obscurity in the mailroom to make him the new fall guy president because he believes Norville is a buffoon and can be manipulated.

The local newspaper, *The Argus*, decides to investigate the new so-called 'Idea Man' further, but Amy Archer, their star reporter, is convinced he is a fraud and goes undercover at The Hud to prove her point.

All of this takes place under the watchful gaze of benevolent old clock keeper Moses and malicious janitor Aloysius, both of whom are far more important, and far more powerful, than their lowly positions would suggest.

Unfortunately for all who wish him ill, Barnes goes on to invent the hula hoop, which is a massive success. Now Mussburger has to destroy Barnes or lose all the power and wealth he has spent his life accumulating...

Commentary: As with all Coen films up to this point (except the determinedly myopic *Barton Fink*), this begins with a landscape and voice-over. In this case, the view is a majestic glide through the towers of Manhattan Island to the grand clock tower of the Hudsucker Building. The narration is provided by Moses, the mysterious keeper of that clock. We are hovering within the confines of the all-important 59th minute, before the 59th year.

'1959, a whole 'nother feelin',' Moses muses. 'The New Year. The future, that's somethin' y' can't never tell about, but the past, well, that's another story!' He then goes on to introduce the idea which this film will explore – the concept of Celestial Mechanics. This is the idea of a regulated, clockwork universe which turns in slow, majestic and meticulously regulated circles. 'Daddy Earth is fixin' to start one mo' trip round the Sun.' The perpetual motion machine that is the universe runs smoothly thanks to powers we can only guess at. Hudsucker Industries, it will transpire, is a key to that process.

Upon considering the celebration of New Year, Moses supposes, 'There's a few lost souls floatin' round out there... outta hope, outta rope, outta time.' For lost souls, read angels... and Norville Barnes. 'How did he get so high, why is he feelin' so low?' The rest of the story answers that question.

As the Khachaturian music swells, so does the hum of the clock. Then the clock rolls back into a flashback. Up in the

Hudsucker Industries boardroom, a glowing year-end report successfully avoids saying what Hudsucker actually produces. This is because The Hud is symbolic of *all* industry, not one in particular.

Downstairs, the divinity that shapes our ends guides the Situations Vacant page to Norville as if drawn by a wire. Norville is then drawn to The Hud. The mechanical universe is slotting into place the cogs of a whole new celestial clock.

Upstairs, Waring Hudsucker seems hypnotised by the distant grey skyscrapers, like magnificent fog-shrouded mausoleums. Taking the trouble to remove, then wind, his pocket watch, he is effectively stepping out of time. As the great Hudsucker clock strikes twelve – the time when everything significant happens at The Hud – Waring Hudsucker hurls himself out of the boardroom window and merges with The Infinite. As he is leaving the penthouse, Norville crosses the pavement and enters through the main doors.

After his boss' untimely departure, we see Sidney Mussburger for the first time, claiming Hudsucker's smouldering cigar, shouldering his responsibilities. His machinations can begin now.

Since The Hud represents the world in microcosm, it has its own legal system. The company by-laws are specific: Hud's kingdom must, in his absence, become a democracy. 'John Q Public' can buy a share in the company, thereby undermining Mussburger's power. As a good dictator, he simply cannot allow this to happen.

Meanwhile, Norville, the unwitting tool of Mussburger's planned triumph, enters the heaving, bustling chaos of the mail room. This maelstrom continues the Coen theme of the dangers of non-communication. Memos and internal mail are the blood flowing through The Hud's veins, all of which require receipts. The pinnacle of this is the dreaded Blue Letter that will become Norville's ticket to the top floor.

On a practical level, these rules and regulations actually prove an obstruction to the smooth running of the business, so they are observed to the letter, but most definitely not to the spirit. 'If you fold [letters] they fire ya. I usually throw em out.' The pragmatic old man who says this is little more than a machine, repeating the same simple act at an inhuman pace.

Of course, it would hardly be a Coen film if the machines that so perfectly represent the order of things didn't complain about it. The Hud clock rumbles and The Hud elevator whines as it speeds away, leaving Norville trapped on the top floor.

Here we meet Aloysius. He is calmly erasing Hudsucker's name from his office door. He erases memory, he takes away the past, because in business, there is no relevant past there is only glorious present. Past victories stand for nothing if they are not followed by present victories. This is why, after 30 seconds of silent contemplation (for which the staff are docked), Waring Hudsucker, founder, president and namesake of The Hud, is effectively forgotten.

Aloysius is the right arm of Mussburger, the dark prince of The Hud. When Norville waves his blue letter at Mussburger's secretary, her scream is described in the script as 'The sound of a million souls moaning in Purgatory.' And if Purgatory is the antechamber, then the main office must be... a return to one of the key themes of *Barton Fink.*·

Apart from his desk, the only furniture in Mussburger's vast office is the globe, indicating the size of the Hud's market, and a ticker-tape machine, telling him the state of that market. This ticks constantly, like a clock. The executive toy on his desk also ticks. Both marking Hudsucker Time!

Norville shows the big man his Big Idea, the one he has been working on 'for the past two or three years.' It takes that long to boil an idea down to the simple perfection of a circle on paper. 'You know, for kids!'

Of course, the circle is the path followed by clock hands and celestial bodies. It is the shape the universe strives for. It charts the journey this tale will take, beginning and ending on New Year's Eve.

Upon realising the potential this seeming buffoon presents, Mussburger commands, 'Wait a minute!' The ticking balls obediently stop. During this sequence, the script repeatedly describes Mussburger's eyes as 'burning.' This simply enforces the belief that, once again, we are dealing with a Devilish individual. Mussburger has unearthly powers (over his executive toy, at least), yet he is denied the position of God in this self-made world, because of the law of its maker. This would seem to make him Lucifer, determined to rule and remake The Hud in his own image. When, at the end, he finds that he will never rule, his first thought is to plunge Hellwards.

So, if Mussburger is the Devil of this little world within the world, and Aloysius is his Demon, that leaves Moses (note the name) in the good guys' corner. He is the guardian angel of the clock, in charge of keeping the power of good running smoothly. All of which, I suppose, makes Norville the Saviour, the spiritual son of the absent God (Waring Hudsucker) who rises again from his own plunge to (un)certain death to save The Hud from the Devil.

The one and only thing Norville and Mussburger have in common is their 'Big Ideas.' The Bumstead Contract is Mussburger's, 'The most important legal document of my career – I've worked four years on this!' In *Miller's Crossing*, a cigarette burning through paper gives Leo the warning he needs to survive the shoot-out. Here, a cigar sets light to the Bumstead Contract, instigating the film's only extant scene of slapstick and heralding the new age of Norville.

Ironically, given Mussburger's characteristic disregard of all mere workers, his life is saved by the stitching given to him by the diligent generosity of a simple working man, his tailor. For the film's first montage, the Laughing Montage, we segue to this tailor's workshop where new president Norville is dressed up accordingly. This non-verbal sequence has similarities to the mime sequences in Jerry Lewis' film *The Patsy* (1964) which, in turn, owes its inspiration in a large part to Charles Chaplin. Eventually, Norville is alone, laughing by himself in his cold, stark void of an office. Over in his even colder, much darker office, Mussburger too is laughing. The script tells us about him, 'The second hand of the Hudsucker clock rumbles by, sweeping a shadow across the floor. Evil prevails.'

Cut to the editor's office of *The Manhattan Argus*. This is a scruffier, less rigidly organised version of The Hud boardroom. It is filled by a crowd of old men listening to their leader. His two best 'men' are Amy and Smitty, who initially confer and concur but eventually fall into opposition as Amy realises that there is more to life than headlines and Pulitzers.

The film's second mime scene is Amy's pick-up of Norville, helpfully narrated by another Coen standby – the streetwise philosopher – this time in the persons of the cabbies Benny and Lou. Having installed Amy as his secretary, Norville rails at the article she has secretly written about him. The letter he dictates clearly demonstrates his naïvety and his lack of irony. Well, if Norville is too trusting to see through her, Old Moses is too wise not to. From his vantage point, he can see everything. His function is, 'To keep the ol' circle turnin'' This doesn't just mean the clock, this means The Hud. The clock is the key, you see: 'Time is money... and money, it drive that ol' global economy and keeps big daddy Earth a-spinnin' on roun'.' The fate of the Earth is tied to The Hud, much as Charlie Meadows' was tapped into the Earle.

At the ball, the women are almost Pythonesque caricatures, described in the script as 'dowagers of the Margaret

Dumont mould.' Mussburger seems only vaguely aware of the existence of his wife, his mind being occupied full time with the execution of his labyrinthine plans. This is just a foretaste of the bitter irony which awaits him, at midnight. Hudsucker Time.

Over at the balcony, Amy tells Norville about Ann's 440, her favourite bar. '[The people there] don't quite fit in. You'd love it.' Then, by implication, since it is her regular haunt, she feels as though she doesn't fit in either! She entered Norville's life determined to destroy him and ends up inheriting some common humanity from him.

Norville, in return, shows surprising instincts when he discusses karma. 'The great circle of life... what goes around comes around... the great wheel that gives us each what we deserve!' He doesn't seem to consciously believe any of it but maybe being aware of the possibility is enough.

When Norville presents his dingus to the blank-eyed Board, Mussburger states, without a trace of irony, 'Congratulation, kid... you've just reinvented the wheel.' Cue another triumphant montage as the hoops are designed, built, marketed and eventually thrown out as failures. Of course, in a carefully regulated clockwork universe, accidents don't happen. Therefore, one of the cast-off hoops makes its way through the streets to the one receptive mind it needs. It turns out that Norville was right, the hoop *is* for kids. Being childish, he saw its appeal.

Cue yet another montage, this one charting Norville's rise to greatness as witnessed by *The Rockwell Newsreel*, which uses a clock as its logo and emphasises the passage of time with its slogans, 'Tidbits of Time – Tempus Fugit... we kid you not!' The traditional German scientist explains the importance of the dingus in the great global scheme of things: 'It operates on ze same principle zat keeps ze Earth spinning round ze Sun, and zat keeps you from flying off ze

Earth into the coldest reaches of outer space ver you vould die like a miserable svine.' So the hula hoop is symbolic of Celestial Mechanics.

Meanwhile, the great circle keeps on turning. When Mussburger's plan backfires, he is philosophical: 'The music plays, the wheel turns, and our spin ain't over yet.' The ever-whining Addison is less sanguine. Aspiring to follow the great Hud, he hurls himself down the boardroom table with a resigned, 'I'm getting off this merry-go-round.'

But what of Amy? Is she still on the merry-go-round? She has been pushed out of Norville's life now and is reduced to reading about him in her own paper. Soon she can hold her tongue no longer and reminds him of who he was when he arrived in town. He, however, has become corrupted by too much time spent with Mussburger. As she puts it, 'What really hurts is watching you outrun your soul chasing after the money...' He has forgotten that he didn't come up with his Big Idea for the money or the glory. He came up with it... for kids!

In the script for this scene, Norville does another of his pausing/listening acts, claiming that an idea is coming to him, then he loses it. Within minutes, Buzz pitches *his* Big Idea – it's a perfect circle. He pitches it to Norville exactly as Norville pitched his idea to the Board. The idea is so similar to Norville's, maybe it is the idea he missed in his office. It just passed him by and bestowed itself upon Buzz instead. After all, ideas are fairly arbitrary things and can come from the most unlikely sources.

But the tide has turned against Norville, as tides inevitably will. Still pursuing his original plan, Mussburger is gathering evidence against Norville. 'There's no second chances,' he assures Norville, 'When you're dead, you stay dead. Just ask Waring Hudsucker.' Well, did Mussburger but know it, Norville will soon learn that Hudsucker has decided, almost as his dying wish, to change this rule of business once and for all. Redemption provides that second chance to the fallen! It is demonstrable of the Coens' restraint that this tale of the fall and rebirth of a leader, which takes place at the end of December, has no specific reference to Christmas. Their inspiration leans more towards the Old Testament.

Lost and alone, Norville wanders through the snow, drowning his sorrows. When he arrives at Ann's 440, he is about as far from his true self as he can get. He has travelled from the progenitor of the perfect circle to, 'Man, he's from squaresville.'

The media's depiction of him has gone full circle – now everyone is printing the story that Amy saw from the start, except she is now too subjective to think it's worth crucifying a person for a headline. She has gone the opposite way to Norville, from cynic to soulful.

Upstairs, the board are sitting. Mussburger finally reveals the extent of his ambition – remaking the world after his own image, renaming the company: Sidsucker Industries. To this end, Aloysius is already painting his name on Norville's door.

And so the tale has turned full circle. We are back at the beginning. Norville steps out onto the ledge and prepares to join with the Infinite. The time for pretence is past, Aloysius flexes his supernatural muscles, blowing at Norville through the window, which clouds with his breath. The force magically passes through the glass and pushes Norville off into the void.

This is a moment for decisive action. Moses stops the clock. He turns to the camera and addresses the viewer directly. He knows he's a character in a story: 'Strictly speakin',' I'm never s'posed to do this.' As Norville hangs suspended, the snow keeps falling, possibly because it is still in mid-air, not part of the Earth yet, and therefore not party to its rules. Neither is Moses. Neither is Aloysius. It is clear that an unspoken animosity exists between these two.

Given this temporary hiatus in the smooth running of the great Celestial Machine, Hudsucker takes the opportunity to come down and address Norville. He describes death as having 'joined the organisation upstairs, an exciting new beginning.' Of course, standard Christian dogma would have it that suicides don't go to Heaven – they lower the tone – but maybe the rules are negotiable if your building is home to the mainspring of the Universe.

It transpires that Hud killed himself over the emptiness of his life. 'My vanity drove away she who could have saved me.' He loved Mussburger's monstrous wife. He was human after all. This is maybe why he sees Mussburger as 'a balls to the wall businessman... very effective.' Mussburger, at heart, isn't human – he never loved his wife because love isn't good business.

As Norville reads out the long-forgotten Blue Letter, he stumbles over the word 'memories.' After all, holes in time are not what memories are made of. 'The new president must be free to fail and learn, to fall and rise again by applying what he has learned. Such is business. Such is life. Failure should never lead to despair, for despair looks only to the past. The future is now, and when our president needs it, Waring Hudsucker hereby bequeaths him his second chance. Long live the Hud.'

So it is written. According to Hud's new law, Hudsucker Industries' new messiah is bequeathed his resurrection. Norville survives the plunge. So the circle has turned. As Moses resumes his narration, it is Mussburger standing out on the ledge (having left his wristwatch behind, of course). Meanwhile, Norville, once again in touch with his inner child, has adapted his perfect circle idea – it now represents the Frisbee.

Moses concludes with the assurance that, however complete a story may feel, there is always room for another spin of the wheel: 'There was a man who threw hisself off the 45th floor, but that's another story.'

Family: None. The motivation of most of the characters here is the void in their lives that a family/relationship would fill. Hudsucker remained forever unfulfilled, despite all of his conquests, because of an unrequited love. Mussburger has no void because he is all business. He is married but hardly notices – the bitter irony being that his marriage is what brings about his downfall. The board members have no personality because they are all business. The only pleasure and pain their mean, soulless lives ever experience is mediated entirely by the share price. Reagan and Thatcher would be proud of them. Amy spends all of her work time denying that she is a woman, while her free time is spent with the outcasts and losers amongst whom she feels at home. Norville loses his way when he leaves his family home, and it is only when he accepts the love of a good woman that he finds his own personality again.

So this film is much more about the effects the absence of family can have on your mental state and your behaviour.

Dreams: After Amy says she loves him, Norville has the dream about the elusive dancer, dressed in flowing red veils, who stays forever out of his reach. This is his relationship with Amy but also his failure to fulfil his potential. He has allowed himself to wallow in the glory of his one Big Idea, rather than keeping in touch with that part of him which created it.

Fargo (1996)
'And for what? For a little bit of money!'

Cast: Frances McDormand[5] (Marge Gunderson), William H Macy (Jerry Lundegaard), Steve Buscemi[4] (Carl Showalter), Peter Stormare[1] (Gaear Grimsrud), Kirstin Rudrüd (Jean Lundegaard), Harve Presnell (Wade Gustafson), Tony Denman (Scotty), Steven Reevis (Shep), Bruce Campbell[3] (Guy on TV)

Crew: Director: Joel Coen, Producer: Ethan Coen, Writers: Joel & Ethan Coen, Cinematographer: Roger Deakins[3], Music: Carter Burwell[6], Editor: Roderick Jaynes[4], Colour, 98 minutes

Plot: Car salesman, Jerry Lundegaard hires the volatile Carl Showalter and the positively volcanic Gaear Grimsrud to kidnap his wife, Jean. His plan is that the kidnap should be non-violent and that his father-in-law, Wade Gustafson, will willingly hand over the $1 million ransom. It doesn't go quite as planned.

Soon, Chief of Brainerd Police Department, Marge Gunderson is investigating a triple homicide. Thus, the peace and quiet of Brainerd has been shattered and the extremely pregnant Marge has to investigate a case where the body count increases daily...

Commentary: Although *Fargo* received the great reviews the Coens were accustomed to, and garnered another heap of trophies, it is the least Coenical of all their films. The narrative is linear, there are no flashbacks, dream sequences, biblical references or bizarre camera techniques.

It is as though, after the critical and commercial failure of *The Hudsucker Proxy*, the brothers retreated to a place, a genre and a cast that they knew and loved. Falling back on a practice they had established when experimenting with Super8 as children, they decided to remake a classic film. In this case, that film was *Blood Simple*.

Like *Blood Simple*, *Fargo* examines the darkness of the human psyche, trapped in a situation from which the only escape seems to be through violence and betrayal. Both films feature husbands who set imbalanced killers on their wives. Both feature Frances McDormand in a leading role. In her speech at the Oscars, McDormand remarked that this was '...the first time in 12 years of sleeping with the director, that I got the job, no questions asked.'

Whereas *Blood Simple* was set in the hot and sweaty wildernesses of Texas, *Fargo*'s long, bleak highways cut indistinct pathways through the windswept snowscapes of Minnesota. A crisp, bleached backdrop against which the stain of mindlessly-shed blood seems all the more vivid.

With typically elliptical logic, the brothers decided to name this film after the town of Fargo where the initial meeting between Jerry, Carl and Gaear takes place, rather than after the town of Brainerd where the rest of the action actually takes place. Traditional Aristotelian rules of dramatic structure demand that, since we start in Fargo, we must return there for the showdown, right? But this isn't drama, it's a true story, beginning with the inter-title, 'This story is true... At the request of the survivors, the names have been changed. Out of respect for the dead, the rest has been told

JOEL AND ETHAN COEN

exactly as it occurred.' So the rest of the film is stubbornly set in either Minneapolis, or the small peaceful town of Brainerd or on the road in between.

Fade to white. Slowly, we realise that we aren't looking at a pure white screen, but at a snow-covered landscape. An ominous black bird circles overhead. Initially, there is no boundary between the snow-covered ground and the low sky. We are already lost. Then a distant car appears, ploughing purposefully into this featureless nowhere. The car's driver, Jerry Lundegaard, believes he is taking steps to regain control of his life but he has wandered far from the beaten track into a world where he has no control whatsoever.

Jerry is a saggy-faced car salesman, as out of place in his several-sizes-too-big windcheater as he is in a bar hiring kidnappers. And so the game is afoot. From his first shambling entrance, Jerry is identifiable of the typical Coenical leading man – none too smart, and wandering haphazardly into the path of a vortex of violence which circumstance and misunderstanding will whip up for him.

The reason why Jerry needs the money is never explained (as with Bernie Birnbaum's double-dealing in *Miller's Crossing*, the debt is the Macguffin, it exists purely as motive). However, he is bullied by his father-in-law, Wade, and overruled by his wife, Jean, so he cuts a rather pathetic figure in his own home. Jean and Jerry must, at one time, have been a perfect couple, since she is so wonderfully unsullied by imagination. As she sits, knitting and watching TV, she spies a man in a black mask looking through her window. She looks at him as though her window was another TV screen, with a different drama unfolding on it. It is not until the masked man breaks the window and invades her space that she jumps up, screaming. In contrast to Carl's characteristically loud entrance, Gaear just opens the front door and grabs her. She bites him, then escapes to the bathroom, as Abby did in *Blood*

Simple. But, unlike Abby, who managed to escape out of the window, Jean can't and hides behind the shower curtain instead.

Gaear has already lost interest in finding her and is seeking ointment for his bleeding finger. Then he realises that they haven't checked the shower curtain. Jean rips the curtain from its hooks and charges for the stairs where she trips, falls head over heels and lays unconscious at the bottom, neatly wrapped up. Carl and Gaear have accomplished the deed without laying a finger on her.

Earlier, in the car, on the way to kidnap Jean, Carl had talked non-stop, Gaear sitting in stony silence. Where Carl will panic and allow confusion to cloud his judgement, Gaear doesn't hesitate. If something isn't going according to plan, he kills someone. Simple yet effective. At least in the short term.

Jerry arrives home, sees the trail of destruction through the house and looks visibly shocked. He clearly never thought that kidnapping his wife would actually involve violence. Still, he deals with his shock and rehearses his grief-stricken phone call to Wade. Once perfected, he calls up, only to be put on hold by the receptionist. It is these moments, observing the pure ludicrousness of life, that make *Fargo* such a unique film – a grim black comedy where, a third of the way through, the heroine still hasn't appeared.

Cut to the Coens' traditional standby – the lonely, unlit highway. Carl has forgotten to change the dealer licence plates on the car Jerry had given them, so they are flagged down by a state trooper. Carl turns to Gaear, who still hasn't said a word, and tells him to leave all the talking to him. Carl's words don't impress the trooper, nor does his bribe. Gaear decides to go down the simple and reliable route of putting one in the brain. Blood spurts like a fountain, covering Carl.

This sparks off a scene lifted almost bodily from *Blood*

Simple, as Carl's roadside corpse-dragging antics are interrupted by an oncoming vehicle. Gaear again takes control, coming to his usual decision, and pursues the witnesses along the empty highway until panic sends them into a skid. It must be his lucky day. This is the second time he has succeeded without having to try. He casually shoots the witnesses dead.

With the body count now up to three, it's about time to call in the police. The phone rings and Officer Marge Gunderson is informed of the triple homicide to which her response is, 'Oh jeez.' Her husband, Norm, insists on getting up and fixing her breakfast. This scene of tediously blissful domesticity introduces the three most important ingredients in Marge's life: her loving and safe marriage to wildlife artist Norm; her seven-month pregnancy; and food. The only occasions where Norm and Marge are seen together, they are either sleeping together or eating together.

Out at the crime scene, Marge and her deputy carry out an analysis of the situation in a very matter-of-fact manner, as though triple homicides were a common occurrence in Brainerd. Through her analysis of the crime scene she immediately and accurately describes the scenario and the sizes for the two culprits. Elementary, my dear Gunderson.

Marge is no fast talking career gal who thinks she's one of the boys. She is a kind, considerate, loyal woman who just happens to be a police chief. There are no gender politics at play. She doesn't have to play any games. It is this combination of her career, her role as wife and rapidly-approaching role of a mother that make Marge such an interesting and challenging role.

Marge and Norm are asleep when the phone rings again, but this time it is not further murders, it's Mike Yanagita, an old university friend. He says that he has seen Marge on TV in connection with the murders and thought he'd call her up.

For the viewer to hear about this TV appearance, rather than see it, is another example of the Coens not playing by the rules of the police procedural yarn. The police chief's moment in the spotlight is an essential standby in such narratives – but not here. In a Coen film, it is more important that a long-dead friendship be embarrassingly reawakened by the glare of the publicity which we are oblivious to.

Marge and Mike meet up. This scene is the only one in which Marge can be herself, away from her husband and her job. However, the scene sits at odds with her character and the mood of the rest of the film. She is understandably uncomfortable when Mike breaks down and cries after telling her about the death of his wife. Marge resists the temptation to 'mother' him and simply gets up and leaves. The next day, when she finds out Mike was lying, her only response is the now familiar, 'Jeez.'

Motivated by Marge's inquiries, Shep, who was the initial contact between Jerry and Carl, pays a visit to Carl and kicks him around the room. Enraged by this, Carl takes his temper out on the only person he has any power over: Jerry. He calls him and demands all the money (thinking that all the money is $80,000). Unfortunately, Wade had been listening in, and takes matters into his own hands.

Carl, unhinged after his beating, is now confronted with Wade, brandishing a gun and demanding to see his daughter. With a factory chimney behind him, roaring like *Blood Simple*'s furnace, Carl, in a moment that is pure Gaear, shoots Wade. But, like Julian Marty before him, Wade won't go down without a fight. Wade shoots at Carl, catching him messily across the side of his jaw. I suppose that's one way of shutting him up.

Spouting blood everywhere, Carl takes the bag full of money (a full million dollars, of course) and drives down the slope to take his temper out on a jobsworth car park attendant. It is at this moment that Jerry's ham-fisted plan, weighed down by the usual concoction of lies, misunderstanding and raw, uncut stupidity, plunges to its nadir. The money is gone. Carl is gone. Wade is gone. Jean is gone. Jerry decides it's time he was gone too. As he disappears down one of those featureless highways, two other car journeys are soon to converge. Firstly there is Carl, discovering the $1 million and deciding to double-cross his silent partner. He buries the money in the snow, beside the road, up against a post of an infinitely long fence. Secondly, there is Marge, returning home to Brainerd.

When Carl returns to the hut, Gaear is engrossed in a drama unfolding on the TV screen – he has no interest in the real-life drama going on around him in much the same way Jean had, at first, only a voyeuristic interest in her own kidnapping. Television is the great sedative, putting everyone to sleep, be they police chiefs or homicidal maniacs.

Carl looks at Jean's body on the ground and enquires what happened to her. Gaear states, matter-of-factly, 'She started shrieking, you know.' Carl doesn't inquire what he did to make her shriek. He genuinely doesn't care. All he can think about, is the money. He seems to momentarily forget the small matter of his little nest egg buried in the middle of nowhere, and starts to bicker with Gaear over ownership of the cursed car Jerry gave them. This exchange forms the dark, comic heart of the film – it exposes the depth of Carl's incalculable greed and galactic stupidity, as well as Gaear's chilling single-minded simplicity. Like the giant statue of Paul Bunyon they have passed so many times, Gaear grabs an axe and uses it on Carl.

Gaear's luck seems to have abandoned him. By the time Marge passes, following up one final clue, and spotting that damned car parked at the hut, he is industriously feeding Carl into the woodchipper.

How does he react to the spectre of this little pregnant woman with a gun? Inexplicably, he turns on his heels and runs. So, Marge gets her man, locking him up in the back of her prowler, and tries to understand how people could be motivated into creating such mindless violence for a little bit of money. Gaear looks longingly at the figure of Paul Bunyon yet remains silent, as silent as a statue.

Marge travels back down the road Jerry took at the beginning of the film. His search for happiness took him out to find corruption and violence. Her search for happiness leads her back home to honest work and family.

As the police arrest Jerry, he, like his wife, tries to escape out the bathroom window. He, like his wife, fails.

And so ends the movie where the two sides of the American dream are played out. The Lundegaards, motivated by money and power, are all dead, jailed or traumatised. The Gundersons, whose life is devoted to simple pleasures, are happily dreaming of a beautiful future for their unborn child. Thus showing that money, even a little bit of money, is not worth selling out for.

Do we get a hint of the Brothers Coen admonishing themselves for dealing with the big Hollywood boys on *The Hudsucker Proxy*?

Note: About six months after the film's release, a vicious rumour began circulating that *Fargo* was, in fact, not a true story at all, but a work of complete fiction. A quote, supposedly from Joel Coen, was sent across the world's media: '...contrary to what it says at the beginning of *Fargo*, it's all made up.' Unfortunately, five years on, this message still hadn't got through to everyone. In November 2001, the Minnesotan paper *Bismarck Tribune* reported that a Japanese woman had been found dead by the village of Detroit Lakes, which is on the road between Fargo and Brainerd. Takako Konishi had allegedly arrived in the area a few days previously, carrying a hand-drawn map and explaining, with the little English she had, that she was searching for buried treasure. On June 6, 2003, *The Guardian* printed a follow-up piece by Paul Berczeller: '… I went to North Dakota to make a film about Takako's 'true story' for Channel 4. My idea was to reconstruct the last week of Takako's life using still photographs, mixed with some digital video, in a kind of contemporary response to Chris Marker's legendary 1964 film roman short, *La Jetée*. I was going to interview the people she encountered along the way, hoping to excavate the real story and the real person beneath the urban myth. The interesting thing – or what I hoped would be interesting – was that the eyewitnesses would then recreate those encounters on film, 'playing' themselves across from an actress (Mimi Ohmori) playing Takako.' The resulting 25 minute film is called *This is a True Story*. And so art becomes life becomes art.

Families: In most crime genre movies, the detective doesn't have a private life and if they do it is one full of disillusionment and neglect. Detectives are so focused on the violent world they inhabit that the thought of bringing a child into that world is abhorrent. Marge is quite different, even though her advanced pregnancy goes virtually without comment throughout the film. Indeed, it isn't even mentioned in the dialogue, until the final scene. Marge does her job, as Chief of Police, during the day, but leaves it in the top drawer of her desk along with the crumbs of that day's doughnuts. She doesn't take any of the emotional baggage or trauma of her work into the happy comfortable home life she shares with Norm.

The heart of the film is Marge and Norm's marriage. Their world is steady, safe and predictable. They are contented with one another. When he tells her of his partial triumph – one of his paintings is to be used on a 3¢ stamp, not the more popular 29¢ he was hoping for – she congratulates him and consoles him. Her solving seven homicides is not mentioned.

Unlike the Lundegaards' male-dominated family, the Gundersons' world is supremely feminine. Norm's career as a wildlife artist fits in around Marge's role as Police Chief. He sees his role as providing food, warmth and love for the hard-at-work breadwinner, and he is deeply content with his role. Although Marge is tempted to meet up with her old flame Mike, as though her comfortable life is in need of spice, the reality of that meeting makes her appreciate her quiet husband all the more.

In contrast, the Lundegaards' lives are dominated by the need for money and status and Jerry's unexpressed rage at having his breadwinning role constantly undermined by his father-in-law. He's worried about money and uses his wife and son as bargaining chips when negotiating with Wade. There is no sense of family within the Lundegaard/Gustafson household. Wade has provided for his daughter and grandson, but not Jerry. Therefore, Jerry's scam is his way of regaining his masculinity and independence. Ironically, in order to free himself of Wade, he has to steal the money from Wade.

Being of immigrant stock, Wade represents the American pioneer, building himself up from nothing, following in the grand tradition of Nathan Arizona, Jack Lipnick and Waring Hudsucker, to name but three. He is a man of action and never doubts the decisions he makes. Unlike Jerry, whose constant prevarication and self-loathing ensure his failure.

Although claiming to be raising the money for Jean and Scotty's benefit, he doesn't really see them as anything more than assets to raise money against. He doesn't imagine or care that Jean's life could ever be put at risk. Throughout the film, his relationship with his son also deteriorates. They start off talking to one another face to face but, by the end, they are shouting to each other from different floors. Then, ultimately, in the most pernicious act a parent can perform, he abandons his son altogether. And for what? For a little bit of money!

Dreams: The family who were dreaming of 29¢ end up with 3¢ and are content; whilst the family who already had a million, end up in a nightmare scenario where they no longer even have each other.

The Big Lebowski (1998)
'That rug really tied the room together, did it not?'

Cast: Jeff Bridges (The Dude), John Goodman[3] (Walter), Julianne Moore (Maude), Steve Buscemi[5] (Donny), David Huddleston (The Big Lebowski), Philip Seymour Hoffman[1] (Brandt), Sam Elliot (The Stranger), Tara Reid (Bunny), Peter Stormare[2] (Uli), John Turturro[3] (Jesus), David Thewlis (Knox Harrington), Ben Gazzara (Jackie Treehorn), Jon Polito[2] (Private Snoop)

Crew: Director: Joel Coen, Producer: Ethan Coen, Writers: Joel & Ethan Coen, Cinematographer: Roger Deakins[4], Music: Carter Burwell[7] & T Bone Burnett[1], Editors: Roderick Jaynes[5] & Tricia Cooke[1], Colour, 126 minutes

Plot: Little Jeffrey Lebowski, known to his friends, his enemies and his total strangers as The Dude, is violently mistaken for Big Jeffrey Lebowski. The result being one pissed-on rug and one pissed-off rug owner.

When The Dude tells his bowling buddies Walter and Donny about it, Walter starts bellowing about drawing a line in the sand. So, The Dude doesn't let it go and is consequently sucked into a whirlwind of violence and intrigue featuring a mad vaginal artist, Maude Lebowski, and a mad vaginal pornographer, Jackie Treehorn.

In between, he fits in a little bowling, a confrontation with his nemesis – the mad bowler Jesus Quintana – and a few curiously calming conversations with the mysterious moustachioed Stranger...

Commentary: This film really ties together everything we have been looking at so far. It involves Chandler, Heaven and Hell, fragile masculinity and dysfunctional families.

Our tale begins by following a tumbling tumbleweed, from the wilderness '...way out West,' momentarily fooling the viewer into thinking that this is going to be a Western (the typeface of the titles would support this), until the brush crests the hill and rolls down towards modern LA.

The Texans of *Blood Simple* talked the talk, while the gangsters of *Miller's Crossing* walked the walk, but it took Hi McDunnough to give it a name, 'I come from a long line... of frontiersmen and outdoor types!' The self-made millionaires, who pepper Coen films, seem to represent the success story of the frontiersman spirit, and it all stems from Western movies.

In essence, this tumbleweed is the spirit of the Old West visiting the New. It makes its way from the wilderness to travel unmolested through the streets of LA, until it arrives at the beach – following the fortunes of one who is almost as rootless and free-spirited as it is...

And here he is, shambling into the dairy department of his local Ralph's: The Dude, '...high in the runnin' for laziest [man] worldwide.' Little does he know that the first of several welcoming committees is lying in wait in his house. These invaders introduce a theme of crude masculinity which will run through the film like... a river of piss. Taking a leak on The Dude's carpet is a primitive, male, territorial act, from which his only recourse is retaliation. But first, a spot of bowling.

Everyone seems to have channelled their sexual energy into this seemingly innocuous game. Which, in the case of Jesus the pederast, is a godsend. The Dude doesn't need women in his life, but this doesn't make him immune when opportunity presents itself. Walter is still completely under the rule of his ex-wife. And Donny? Well, he doesn't demonstrate any sexual awareness at all.

The language they employ indicates that bowling is life and death to them – and they play as they live. Donny is quiet and simple. For Walter, bowling is war. 'This is not 'Nam, this is bowling. There are rules!' He insists Smokey crossed the toe line and he is big on drawing lines. The language is also forcibly masculine. 'I don't wanna be a hard-on about this,' laments the put-upon Smokey.

There's a lot of aggressively homophobic energy here, especially from Jesus: 'Are you ready to be fucked, man?... you flash a piece on the lanes, I'll take it away from you and stick it up your ass and pull the fucking trigger till it goes 'click'!' All of which is immediately preceded by the delightful sight of him and partner, Liam, polishing their balls.

Balls are, of course, synonymous with masculinity. Indeed, plenty of screen time dwells on the very sexual nature of bowling itself. Jesus enters the film in extreme close-up, licking his bowl, which is pink. Then there are the sensual slow-motion montages of men sliding fingers into holes, followed by an energetic build-up, a quick release and a crashing climax.

Beyond its purpose as sexual metaphor, bowling plays a crucial role in this movie as cheap therapy. In a world that otherwise frustrates them, Walter and The Dude are extremely comfortable at the alley where the rules are simple. As The Dude journeys back and forth between Venice Beach, Malibu and Pasadena, and as he shifts from drop-out to detective, the bowling alley becomes an island of sanity, more homely than home. There are neon stars on the walls, implying that this is a world, even a universe, all of its own.

The official Big Lebowski web site, which employed the conceit of being written by The Dude, summarised the game thus: 'Bowling is the sport of the social American and has remained unchanged for millions of years... On a nightly basis... [we] arrange our problems and metaphysical contradictions into neat rows and knock the Hell out of them. It's primeval, man... deeply satisfying.'

There is something primeval about the Big L's, 'Seclusion in the west wing.' The room in which he skulks is church-like, with tented arches, deep moody shadows and the German opera *Die Tote Stadt* howling in the background. The room is lit solely from a Hellish fire roaring in the grate.

On Big L's trophy wall, pride of place goes to a photo of him with Mrs Reagan. Of course, the fact that it is *Mrs* Reagan symbolises his emasculation. As, for that matter, do the Urban Achievers, his surrogate children. Therefore, when he rhetorically asks The Dude, 'What makes a man? Is it being prepared to do the right thing? Whatever the price?' The Dude's response, 'Sure, that and a pair of testicles,' is not the reassurance he was looking for. In fact, Big L is here hinting at the lengths to which he will go to get some financial independence – much like Jerry Lundegaard before him.

Meeting Maude Lebowski is an experience only the drug-inundated could successfully handle. She paints a snow angel by flying Harpy-like overhead, nude, in a bondage harness, panting and squealing and dribbling paint across the floor – all very sexual... if you're into that sort of thing.

When talking, Maude emphasises sexual terms like, 'withdrawal' and 'banging... to use the parlance of our times.' Dollars are, "Bones' or 'Clams' or whatever you call them.' Then she proudly proclaims, 'Vagina. The word itself makes some men uncomfortable... [they] find it difficult to say. Whereas, without batting an eye, a man will refer to his 'dick' or his 'rod' or his 'Johnson.'" Just as with the men on the lanes, her dialogue suggests her sexual starvation.

Much later, basking in a post-coital haze, The Dude mixes himself a Caucasian and reassures her that he is sticking to a 'strict drug regimen to keep the brain limber.' When he hears that Lebowski has no money, the cogs in his dope-fuelled brain fall into place. Big L never had any money and was never in charge, hence his wounded libido's need for the trophy wife. 'Father's weakness is vanity. Hence the slut,' confirms Maude, lying naked in The Dude's bed.

'I love you,' The Dude tells Walter, without a trace of the *double entendre* this would entail within the bowling alley environment, 'But sooner or later you're gonna hafta face the fact – you're a goddam moron!' Thanks to Walter's intervention, the ransom drop is botched and The Dude loses his cool, becoming, 'Very un-Dude.'

This is because the situation is frighteningly real. He is suddenly responsible for somebody else's well-being and can't cope with that. 'Her life was in our hands!' He becomes catatonic and in this state, he leaves the money in the car, which chooses this moment to get itself stolen.

In short order, The Dude finds his toes, then his 'Johnson,' under threat of castration. Well, that kind of macho aggression can ruin your whole day. Ask Julian Marty. Understandably, not even a chilled Caucasian can compensate, 'I *could* be sittin' here with just pee stains on my rug.' But, of course, he had to listen to Walter's advice. 'I need my fucking Johnson!' he rages. Donny, ever the innocent, wonders, 'What do you need that for, Dude?'

Cue The Stranger in his snowy white hat, wafting in on a breeze, like the tumbling tumbleweed. A sagely and somewhat lenient representation of the frontiersman spirit, The

Stranger smiles paternally at The Dude and reminds him, 'Sometimes y' eat the bar, and sometimes the bar, wal, he eats you!' After this brief, seemingly meaningless exchange, The Dude's spirits seem to pick up.

It is apparent that someone, somewhere, is watching over The Dude's adventures. Not just his ever-present tail, DaFino the Detective, and not just this Stetson-wearing fairy godfather. As The Dude has the revelation that Big Lebowski kept the million for himself, the viewers are treated to a flashback of Big L not putting the money in the briefcase. This shot is ominously lit and with the action being looked down upon, as if someone above were taking an interest. Whoever is looking after The Dude's well-being, he most certainly moves in mysterious ways.

And so The Dude is summoned to the fiery pits of Hell. Or Malibu, as the locals call it. The official web site pulls no punches in its depiction of Treehorn's playground: 'Malibu is doomed. God has tried everything. Burning it with fires, washing it away with floods and concealing it with mud. Despite His best efforts, they just keep rebuilding Malibu. It's definitely Biblical, man.'

Treehorn (great name for a pornographer, by the way) emerges from the flames of a huge bonfire, in the slow motion previously reserved for The Dude's other unholy nemesis – Jesus. He states that his business is, 'Publishing, entertainment, political advocacy.' The latter gives one the disturbing feeling that his and Big L's paths may have crossed in that most legitimate of spheres. Not that politicians would ever dream of getting involved in anything seedy, of course.

Treehorn's house is clearly designed to promote paranoia, having no right angles and no verticals. Yet The Dude is relaxed, and once again adopts his Marlowe demeanour. Once again, he is bribed with a percentage of the million. Once again, he doesn't see a dime.

As detectives go, he is a bit of a disaster – his first attempt at interrogation ended with Walter going mad and his car getting trashed… again. Here, his first attempt at investigation ends with him 'decoding' a doodle of a man with an optimistically huge dick and falling victim to a Mickey Finn.

Like Tom Regan, The Dude constantly loses fights and receives head injuries. One wonders if the job is much the same for DaFino, who chugs around in the trademark private-eye VW, asserts his masculinity by calling himself 'a dick, man,' and comments on the similarity between The Dude's M.O. and Tom Regan's. 'Playing one side against the other… in bed with everybody, fabulous stuff, man!'

And so, in conclusion, the tale does what a Coencoction usually does – it turns full circle. The Dude barges into Big L's palace, demanding, 'Where's the fucking money, Lebowski,' which, under slightly different circumstances, was the film's opening line! Also, Walter finally gets to reclaim some ground for the spirit of Independence – when The Nihilists, in one last ditch attempt to get something for nothing, decide to use out-and-out aggression, something Walter can understand. 'Without a hostage, there is no ransom… those are the fucking rules.' He so wants to live in a world with rules. Here, he gets a chance to enforce a few, drawing his line in that metaphorical sand and defending it. The Dude has lost the most and is willing to write it off. Walter, who has lost nothing, won't.

Screaming 'I fuck you in the ass!' The Nihilists wade in. This is the moment Walter has been waiting for, the justification of all his paranoia and bluster – a moment of raw, primeval violence! Appropriately, he begins by using his bowl as a weapon (as in *Crimewave*) then follows this by biting off an ear (as in Ethan's short story *A Fever in the Blood*).

It is the trauma of witnessing all this violence that kills Donny, not the threat posed by The Nihilists. It turns out that he was the fragile one, not Smokey. As the quote from Psalms 103 verses 15-16 on the funeral parlour wall puts it, 'As for man, his days are as grass; as a flower of the field so he flourisheth, For the wind passeth over it and it is gone.' The picture fades to black, leaving behind the neon stars, then they too are snuffed out with an unearthly moan.

After the sincere, if incompetent, makeshift funeral service, where Walter takes charge once more and The Dude is covered from head to foot in the ashes of his friend, The Dude finally, seismically, loses his temper, 'You fucking asshole... You make everything a fucking travesty.' In the face of this, all of Walter's tightly-restrained insecurities are exposed. The script states, 'Walter, for the first time, is genuinely distressed, almost lost.' The Dude relents. He has said his piece, 'Fuck it, let's go bowling.'

And so they go home. The Dude makes his traditional journey to the bar and orders a soda, not a White Russian. Maybe he's seen the error of his lazy ways... for a while. The camera pulls back to reveal The Stranger, perched on a bar stool, sizing up a Sioux-City sarsaparilla. The tumbleweed's 'stupefyin'' journey has come to an end. Like Moses in *The Hudsucker Proxy* before him, he turns and addresses the viewer directly, 'It's good knowin' he's out there, The Dude, takin' her easy for all us sinners.' His role is to wind things up, emphasise the completeness of the story, and maybe dribble a little irony into the cracks because, you see, Maude is apparently pregnant after all. 'I guess that's the way the whole durned human comedy keeps perpetuatin' itself, down through the generations, westward the wagons, across the sands of time...'

Of course, what I want to know is – what about The Dude's rug?

Families: As soon as the tale shifts to The Big Lebowski's mansion, the importance of family becomes a key theme.

Brant confides that the Urban Achievers are, 'Mr Lebowski's children, so to speak...' In compensation for his one contemptuous daughter, he has resorted to 'buying' a huge new family.

We are introduced to Big L's mansion with a close-up of The Dude's face reflected in one of his namesake's awards. This reflection speaks to a bond between them, as between Hi and Lenny in *Raising Arizona*. After all, Big L is the one who evokes The Dude's parents: 'Do what your parents did – get a job, sir!'

There are other links between the two Lebowskis, 'some Chinaman in Korea' took Big L's legs, just as a Chinaman ('Dude, Chinaman is not the preferred uh...Asian-American. Please.') peed on The Dude's rug. Granted, the two events are of vastly different scales, but coincidences don't happen by accident! Secondly, The Dude parks his car in the disabled zone, which has an icon of a stick figure in a wheelchair painted onto the tarmac – again linking this Lebowski to the other.

'It is a male myth about feminists that we hate sex,' Maude insists. 'It can be a natural, zesty enterprise.' Yet, when she shows The Dude the porno movie, she clearly has no under-standing of its purpose, merely commenting that the story is 'ludicrous.' Much later, after responding to her mechanical demand, 'Love me,' he could be forgiven for thinking that her frigid exterior had momentarily melted because of the heat of her passion. Of course, it was actually far more contrived than that. 'What did you think this was about, fun and games?' It's at this point you realise that, whilst insisting that feminists can enjoy sex, she never actually committed to an opinion on it herself. Obviously, there must be a maternal-istic need in there somewhere. She presumably selected The Dude because he is the only healthy heterosexual she knows. Shame he's her brother!

Then there is the small matter of The Dude's other 'family.' Even the Coens in interview, admit that The Dude and Walter quarrel 'like an old married couple,' which, by extension, makes Donny their son. Donny is certainly the innocent, his understanding is restricted purely to issues relating to bowling. The Dude and Walter deliberately talk over his head – literally, when at the bar. Visually, he is completely clean shaven and seems to have a hint of acne – the other two have beards. Also, he is the only one who actually seems to play. The other two just seem to go to the alley to absorb the ambience.

In conversation, Walter is particularly vicious to Donny, sometimes shockingly so, yet he protects him from the meaning of the word 'pederast' and, when under threat from the Nihilists, reassures him, 'They won't hurt us, Donny. These men are cowards.' This inconsistency is typical of bad parenting.

Dreams: The Dude experiences his first hallucination after lying on his rug, listening to the restful sound of bowling and looking forward to the Dylan on the reverse side of the tape.

Both of these sound sources feed into his dream as his mind explores his fear of the situation he is in. He isn't in control, he is miniaturised and in the path of a bowl Maude has rolled. Assuming a suspiciously phallic pose, he finds himself wedged inside one of the bowls' finger-holes and, for the first time, sees the world from that rather unique perspective.

His second, not unrelated hallucination, draws on the details he has subconsciously picked up on his travels – the diva from Big L's opera, the black and white floor tiles from Big L's palace, the cable engineer from the porn movie and, needless to add, bowling. All of this is mixed in with Saddam Hussein, a wall of shoes leading to the moon, and The

Nihilists dressed in red devil suits, coming to chop off his Johnson with the giant scissors off Maude's studio wall. All mixed up into a soft porn Busby Berkeley dance routine. As with his first dream, he becomes the bowling ball, once he has delicately guided Maude's fingers into the appropriate holes.

No, I think it's fair to say that he had absolutely no sex on his mind that day!

O Brother, Where Art Thou? (2000)

'Well, ain't this place a geographical oddity – two weeks from everywhere!'

Cast: George Clooney[1] (Ulysses Everett McGill), John Turturro[4] (Pete), Tim Blake Nelson (Delmar O'Donnell), John Goodman[4] ('Big' Dan Teague), Holly Hunter[3] (Penny), Chris Thomas King (Tommy Johnson), Charles Durning[2] (Menelaus 'Pappy' O'Daniel), Wayne Duvall (Homer Stokes), Michael Badalucco[2] (George 'Babyface' Nelson), Stephen Root[1] (Radio Station Man), Daniel Von Bargen (Sheriff Cooley)

Crew: Director: Joel Coen, Producer: Ethan Coen, Writers: Joel & Ethan Coen, Cinematographer: Roger Deakins[5], Music: Carter Burwell[8] & T Bone Burnett[2] & Chris Thomas King, Editors: Roderick Jaynes[6] & Tricia Cooke[2], Colour, 102 minutes

Plot: In the deep South, in the deep Depression, in the 1930s, three convicts (Ulysses, Pete and Delmar) are fugitives from a chain gang. They are intent on getting to the $1.2 million Ulysses claims he has stashed away in his old homestead. The first of their many problems is the fact that the house, the loot and the surrounding countryside will soon be swept away by a massive flood, created by a new dam.

In their attempt to get across country in time, the three

wanderers encounter the temptations of the flesh, the Devil incarnate and the redemption of baptism, as well as a notorious gangster and the massed ranks of the Ku Klux Klan. Yet they still find time to discredit a local politician and become hit recording artists...

Commentary: As much as it takes its cue from Homer's *The Odyssey*, *O Brother, Where Art Thou?* also owes a very obvious and fond debt to Preston Sturges' comedy *Sullivan's Travels* (1942). That film tells the story of a guilt-ridden film director who wants to make an *important* film, about the reality of poverty. So he ventures out onto the road as a hobo to see what the world is like at ground level. Since he is incapable of coping in the real world of Depression America, he soon finds himself clamped in irons and it is here, in a chain gang, that he realises how escapist movies (musicals, romances, screwball comedies) help to salve the wounds real life inflicts on real people. The *important* film he sets out to make but then rejects when he realises it would merely exacerbate the problems of the poor was to be called *Brother, Where Art Thou?*

Almost 60 years on, here it finally is. Of course in the hands of the Coens it becomes something quite different. Part political satire, part slapstick comedy, part fantasy, part musical, part Homeric pastiche and part Biblical epic, *O Brother, Where Art Thou?* weaves a lightweight fabric that seems fairly insubstantial, until one considers its details carefully.

It could be argued that colour is very important in the Southern USA. The colour of your money and the colour of your skin. As good Jewish boys, the Brothers Coen will have some understanding of racial discrimination and have seen fit to address this issue in this context. However, being the Coens, their take on race is nothing if not... elliptical.

This film starts in black and white, then quickly dissolves

to sepia. A simple and subtle motif that suggests things aren't simply a matter of black and white. This also serves as an experimental foreshadowing of the monochromatic *The Man Who Wasn't There*.

The first people we see are the black prisoners on a chain gang, singing dolefully as they swing their picks. 'Po Lazarus' is an old work song from the plantations, and was recorded by James Carter while he was serving time on a chain gang – it is the only original recording on the film's soundtrack.

Whilst it was certainly the truth for some, this image has become an icon, a stereotypical image of the period taken straight out of films like *I Am a Fugitive From a Chain Gang* (1932) and the aforementioned *Sullivan's Travels*. The idea of dignified black folk patiently singing their way through life's miseries is a symptom of a world as imagined by novelists and film-makers, as opposed to the real experiences of the children of slaves.

So, in the film's opening moments we are given to understand that this isn't the real South of the 1930s, but rather a romanticised, nostalgic version of it. Every colour frame of film has been digitally tinted to heighten this unworldly feel and, as the sepia tone seeps into the trees, turning all their leaves to gold, we hear the strains of 'Sweet Rock Candy Mountain.' This then is a sweet, sugary, artificial world. The sort of place which remains forever two weeks from everywhere.

Our heroes are introduced promptly and in a familiar manner as three prisoners rising from the ground – much as the Snopes boys do in *Raising Arizona*. Their very first encounter (after narrowly missing the train) is with a blind seer, patiently pumping his flatcar down the railroad of life and dispensing wisdom to those who will listen. In a manner not dissimilar to *Hudsucker's* Moses, this old black man has a past-tense perspective on the unfolding events. He assures them they 'Must travel a long and difficult road' and confuses them with the revelation that they will encounter a 'cow on the roof of a cotton house' before their adventures are done. (Another blind man, Mr Lunn at his WEZY radio station, inadvertently brings about the riches the three seek by recording The Soggy Bottom Boys' speciality: 'Songs of salvation to salve the soul.')

The three partners' journey begins, as so many Coen journeys do, with a long, straight road. In this case, a railroad. Later, after Delmar is 'saved,' he describes his future path as 'the straight and narrow.'

Oddly enough, despite their attempts to travel in the shortest, straightest line possible, they seem to be forever turning in typically Coenical circles. More than once they encounter the chain gang from which they so flamboyantly escaped.

The South, whether actual or fantasised, would hardly be The South without a healthy dose of that ole time religion. When Pete calls on his unsentimental cousin, Wash Hogwallop, they find themselves betrayed and trapped in a burning barn. Pete dubs his kin 'Judas Iscariot Hogwallop.' Meanwhile, supervising the attempts to raise fire is an impassive white man with a dog, the flames reflected in his black, blank eyeglasses.

In the deep Depression South, it wouldn't be too great a leap to characterise the Devil as a white man. As Tommy tells them when discussing his recent pact with the Devil: 'He's white - white as you folks, with mirrors for eyes an' a big hollow voice an' allus travels with a mean old hound.' His name, it transpires, is Cooley and for him the three fugitives have a choice: 'It's either the penal farm or the fires of damnation.'

In order to redress the colour balance somewhat, the very next white people the travellers encounter are the binary opposition of the Devil: Emerging like spirits from the mist, a congregation assembles by the riverside. They are, however, heard before they are seen, as their angelic singing wafts into camp and Ulysses asks the most improperly phrased question possible: 'Now what the Hell is that singing?' It is, of course, the voice of redemption. Pete and Delmar both heed the call to baptism and, they believe, wash away their former misdeeds. However, as Ulysses wastes no time in pointing out 'Even if it did put you square with the Lord, the State of Mississippi is more hard-nosed.' Still, he remains philosophical, 'I guess you're my cross to bear.' Little does he know how his own singing voice will lead to a form of redemption with that very same state.

Indeed, by the tale's end, all three men will be born anew in one way or another, their past misdeeds behind them. When Ulysses meets his daughters, they tell him, 'Mama said you was hit by a train.' That being so, he is now a resurrected man, after a fashion. Similarly, they believe Pete was transformed into a toad and then miraculously... wasn't. Of course, in truth he was being tortured by the glass-eyed Devil, Cooley, who throws a noose over a branch and calls it a 'Stairway to Heaven' before a light rain starts to fall 'Like God's own mercy.' That's a rebirth of sorts. And sweet, simple Delmar keeps faith with his desire to stay on the straight and narrow since all his sins were so conveniently washed away. So, in one way or another, they are all resurrected men.

Everyone, it seems, is looking for answers. We are told that Cora Hogwallop ran off to find answers and Ulysses opines over the baptismal choir: 'I guess hard times flush the chumps. Everyone's looking for answers...'

And so, into this religiously rarefied atmosphere, with Pete and Delmar still wet behind the ears from their recent absolving, steps Tommy Johnson. Tommy is living proof that if, as Ulysses believes, being redeemed doesn't make you all good, selling your soul to the Devil doesn't make you all bad.

Of course, it isn't just the Devil hisself who is white: The evildoers throughout this film are white. They actually dress in bleached white in the cases of Homer, 'Big' Dan, and Pappy with his entire entourage and the Ku Klux Klan. Unlike the white-gowned worshippers by the riverside, the white gowns of the choreographed KKK are not a demonstration of inner purity, but rather a symbolic disguise to hide the inner demons. Their burning crucifix is a mockery of the piety of the preacher by the riverside.

Similarly, the three white sirens, singing by the riverside and washing their drawers, are the binary opposite of the baptismal congregation... they are temptation away from Delmar's straight and narrow. They hypnotise Pete, initially, with their lilting 'You and me and the Devil make three.' However, the others fall under their spell with the soothing 'Go to sleep little baby.' The three men, not exactly intellectual giants any of them, obligingly drop off.

There are powerful magics at play in this world and not just those on which men of faith can call. Holding Pete the Toad gingerly in his hands, Delmar says they have to find 'some kinda wizard.' Later, after they are reunited with Pete the not-Toad, they do indeed meet a Grand Wizard... of the KKK.

But, before all this, they encounter far more earthly powers. They are walking along another long straight road when fate and celebrity intervenes in their journey once more in the form of George 'Babyface' Nelson in midgetaway. Making his contribution to the ecclesiastical spirit of the film, he asserts, 'Jesus saves, but George Nelson withdraws... I'm George Nelson. Born to raise Hell!'

He leads the boys into a bank robbery not dissimilar to that enacted by the Snopes in *Raising Arizona*. Here, he clearly demonstrates suicidal tendencies. This might explain why, at the film's close, when he is seen being taken into custody and almost certain death at the head of a column of disgruntled dairy farmers, he couldn't be happier. This is the pinnacle of his career, his proudest moment. For him, the money isn't the point of his crimes – it's the fame. He wants to overcome his crippling feeling of inadequacy by being hunted and feared. When, after the mania, the Depression sets in, he simply wanders off into the anonymity of night.

Not unlike George, the three fugitives simply aren't smart enough to be motivated by money. Ulysses' problem seems to be that he thinks too small. He has the wit and wherewithal to steal Wash's watch, and to invent two extra Soggy Bottom Boys so the blind Mr Lunn will pay them an extra $20, yet he doesn't have the sense to hang on to money when it literally showers down on him.

When George disappears into the dark, he leaves them his 'folding money,' which, although uncounted, doubtless amounts to a considerable fortune. Unfortunately, Ulysses doesn't have the good sense to keep the money from the deceitful clutches of 'Big' Dan Teague, the Bible salesman who hides his corruption behind a facade of altruistic bonhomie... and a white eye-patch. For a man who claims to have no faith in the Lord, Ulysses places far too much faith in a Bible salesman. 'The Truth... Folks are lookin' for answers an' 'Big' Dan Teague sells the only book that's got 'em!' In *Barton Fink* Goodman's Charlie Meadows was a similarly irrepressible, sweaty character, who sold 'peace of mind.' There, as here, his agreeable demeanour hides something dark and ugly which can only be cauterised by fire.

Now, before we move on, let us take a moment to consider the 'Based upon *The Odyssey*' credit. It caused the Brothers Coen some amusement come the Awards season, because the film was variously nominated in Best Original

Screenplay and Best Adapted Screenplay categories, depending on how seriously the various academies took the film. However, unlike the 'based on a true story' nonsense which opens *Fargo*, there actually *is* some basis to the claim that *O Brother* is based on Homer's *Odyssey*.

Firstly there is the fact that the protagonists begin by escaping imprisonment. Then there are the names of Clooney and Hunter's characters – Ulysses and Penelope – and the fact that, upon his return to Ithaca, he must stop her from marrying suitors.

Pappy's first name, Menelaus is also the name of the king of Lacedaemon. The old blind man on the flat bed is an Oracle. The bathing girls in their underwear are a mix of The Lotus-Eaters and their hypnotic spells, and Circe with her entrancing song. They turn Turturro into a toad; in the Homer version, Circe turned Ulysses' men into pigs. The Cyclops, Polyphemus, is blinded by a burning spear; one-eyed 'Big' Dan Teague almost is. Finally, when Ulysses returned to Ithaca, Greece, he did so disguised as an old man; as do The Soggy Bottom Boys when they return to Ithaca, Mississippi.

In a delightful example of lateral thinking, 'Big' Dan is perfect to represent the decent God-fearing fold of the Ku Klux Klan because, along with Wizards, their hierarchy includes the rank of Exalted Cyclops.

Families: Just as The Dude, Walter and Donny were a family, so these three fugitives are a notional kin chained together initially by bonds of iron, but eventually by bonds of loyalty... and stupidity.

The father is Ulysses, ambitious, pompous and, as we later find, a prodigious father in the biological sense. Pete is a little more sensible, is the most put-upon of the three and has the more passive mother role. Delmar is therefore the sweet but dim child, following where the others lead – into criminality and mischief – then taking his own lead when respectability and redemption are offered.

Their blood families are far less reliable to them than they are to each other. Ulysses has told his chain-gang family that he can provide them with untold riches if they follow him. He is lying at the time but a tide of incidents eventually prove his words true and make him a provider for both his families. Of course, his true motive for escaping is the desire to prevent his fantastically fertile wife from forging a whole new family by remarrying. Delmar's motive is simply that he wants to buy back the family farm because 'you ain't no kind of man if you ain't got land.' Pete has no loyalty left for his family. All he wants is to 'go out west somewhere, open a fine restaurant. I'm gonna be the maider dee.'

Ulysses and his wife are about as incompatible as two Homo Sapiens can be. He is (generally) a thoughtful, reasoning man but she is reactionary and obsessive. Their difference is perfectly encapsulated in their attitude towards money. Ulysses, as we've already discussed, doesn't notice a fortune when it's handed to him. His wife, on the other hand, has a much more American attitude towards money. When we first meet her we are told she is 'at the five and dime' and her name is Penny.

Holly Hunter's previous foray into Coen country was as the infertile Ed McDunnough, driven to distraction by her inability to conform with society's expectations of her as a mother. Here, the overly fertile Penny is concerned with society's expectations of her as a *good* mother. She is driven to acquire status, and she needs money to get it. She is ambitious for her family in the only way she knows how. Vernon T Waldrip, her new suitor, is suitably 'bona fide.'

Pappy O'Daniels is similarly a family man but, where Ulysses' children have been taught to be ashamed of him,

Pappy is mortally embarrassed by his stupid children. In which case, it was probably a mistake employing them to run his re-election campaign.

Down From the Mountain (2001)
'Never follow animal acts or kids.'

Crew: Directors: Donn Alan Pennebaker & Nick Doob & Chris Hegedus, Musical Directors: T Bone Burnett[3] & Bob Neuwirth, Concert Producer: Denise Stiff, Producer: T Bone Burnett, Executive Producers: Ethan & Joel Coen, Art Direction: Ethan & Joel Coen & Jim Kemp, Master of Ceremonies: John Hartford. B&W/Colour, 98 minutes

Commentary: While the film *O Brother, Where Art Thou?* came and went without causing too much of a ripple on the surface of public perception, the soundtrack album produced an unprecedented splash.

Essentially a collection of modern takes on old Americana, this mixes elements of bluegrass, country, blues and spirituals to combine new compositions with long-forgotten traditional songs. *O Brother* quietly climbed to the top of the charts and stayed there. Unable to ignore it any longer, the album began to attract the attention of both the mainstream and country music press, which only fuelled its fire and has led to sales of over seven million to date.

Not content with earning lots of money for all concerned (except possibly the long-dead composers), the album won a bucketful of gongs at the 2001 Country Music Awards and then confounded all expectation by being named Album of the Year at the 2002 Grammies.

In one of those life-mirrors-art events which seems to dog the Brothers Coen's career, the fictional Soggy Bottom Boys became a real band, featuring soloist Dan Tyminski (standing in for George Clooney) who won the award for Best Single of the Year with 'Man of Constant Sorrow.' The album also won the Best Album award at the 12th International Bluegrass Music Association Awards.

All of this is remarkable enough but what makes this a truly Coenical story is the fact that, a year before this spectacular success, the Brothers had given their blessing to a gigantic charity hoedown. In May 2000, the soundtracks' performers gathered at the Ryman Auditorium, Nashville, for a one-off musical yee-hah.

This is not, in itself, so unusual. Such events are often organised by film companies as part of the pre-release publicity for a major motion picture. What makes this so prescient, is the fact the D. A. Pennebaker was invited along to film the event. Pennebaker is widely regarded as the godfather of the concert movie, thanks to his pioneering work on Bob Dylan's *Don't Look Back* (1967) and Bowie's *Ziggy Stardust and the Spiders From Mars* (1973). And so, *Down From the Mountain* was born. It had a limited theatrical release in the UK, and is available on DVD and video. The first half features Pennebaker's usual cinéma-vérité observations of the behind-the-scenes preparations for the big event. The rehearsals and backstage gossip leading up to the big night are photographed in a typically grainy style with hand-held cameras. It's all fairly standard-issue MTV-type stuff. The second half of the film, however, is the concert itself.

Since none of the acts are introduced, these great names of country music will, like as not, mean very little to the uninitiated; a matter which is not greatly assisted by the DVD's accompanying handbook, which only lists 12 of the concert's 19 performers... in the wrong order. So, by way of assisting your viewing pleasure, we can confirm that the running order is:

Introduction by Holly Hunter[4]
'Po Lazarus' – The Fairfield Four
'Big Rock Candy Mountain' – John Hartford
'Blue and Lonesome' – Alison Krauss & Union Station with Mike Compton
'Green Pastures' – Emmy Lou Harris and Gillian Welch
'The Indian War Whoop' – John Hartford and Gillian Welch
'Go To Sleep You Little Baby' – Emmy Lou Harris, Gillian Welch and Alison Krauss
'J. L. Burned Down the Liquor Store' – Chris Thomas King and Colin Linden
'I am Weary (Let Me Rest)' – Willard Cox and The Cox Family
'Will There Be Any Stars in My Eyes' – Willard Cox and The Cox Family
'In the Highways' – The Peal Sisters
Intermission
'Down to the River to Pray' – Alison Krauss and choir
'Fiddle Solo' – John Hartford
'My Dear Someone' – Gillian Welch, David Rawlings and John Hartford
'I Want' – Gillian Welch, David Rawlings and John Hartford
'Keep on the Sunny Side' – Buck White and the Whites
'Hotfoot' – John Hartford and Band
'O Death' – Ralph Stanley
'Snow White Wings' – Finale – the entire cast led by Ralph Stanley
End Credits – 'I'll Fly Away' – Alison Krauss and Gillian Welch

The Man Who Wasn't There (2001)
'The more you look, the less you really know.'

Cast: Billy Bob Thornton[1] (Ed Crane), Frances McDormand[6] (Doris Crane), James Gandolfini ('Big' Dave Brewster), Michael Badalucco[3] (Frank Raffo), Jon Polito[3] (Creighton Tolliver), Tony Shalhoub[2] (Freddie Riedenschneider), Scarlett Johansson ('Birdy' Abundas), Richard Jenkins[1] (Walter Abundas)

Crew: Director: Joel Coen, Producer: Ethan Coen, Writers: Joel & Ethan Coen, Cinematographer: Roger Deakins[6], Music: Carter Burwell[9] & Ludwig Van Beethoven, Editors: Roderick Jaynes[7] & Tricia Cooke[3], B&W, 115 minutes

Plot: Santa Rosa in rural California, 1949. Ed Crane is a guilty man. 'Guilty of wanting to be a dry cleaner.' That's the extent of his ambition. Otherwise he is an emotionless and virtually motionless barber. His innocuous, banal plan requires a little bit of money... for investment... and that's why it all goes terribly wrong. Ed is vaguely aware that his wife, Doris, is energetically pursuing an affair with her boss, 'Big' Dave, so he casually decides to blackmail Dave for $10,000.

When Dave realises who is blackmailing him, Ed accidentally and economically kills him, before resuming his humdrum barber's existence. But this is only the beginning.

Ed is the still, calm, eye at the centre of an accumulating maelstrom which spirals around him dragging in his wife, the rest of his family, the police and the casual regard of a passing UFO (well, this is almost the 1950s).

All Ed must do is persuade someone in authority that it wasn't Doris who murdered Dave. They just need to understand that the guilt is his. But no one will believe him. After all it couldn't be Ed because he's the man who wasn't there.

Commentary: The Brothers Coen surprised everyone with this film. A few weeks before its release, it was still being referred to as 'The Barber Project.' When the title was finally revealed, everyone expected the film to carry Hitchcock influences. It does, after a fashion. After all, *Shadow of a Doubt* was also set in Santa Rosa and was made in 1949. Then the knowledge that the film would be presented in black and white and would concern a man who becomes a cuckold, a blackmailer and a murderer, led us to expect a dark, dry-as-firewood Film Noir pastiche.

The Coens were up to their usual trick of confounding expectations. Their previous two films had led audiences to expect a bright and light-hearted comedy. How soon they forget. *The Big Lebowski* had failed to ignite box offices because it was a bright and light-hearted comedy, not a follow-up to the cold and gruesome *Fargo*.

The contrasts between *The Man Who Wasn't There* and *O Brother, Where Art Thou?* could hardly be more marked. From an ensemble piece to a single-minded meditation on solitude. From vivid artificially-enhanced colour to tonal black and white. From Ulysses, a central character who talks incessantly, to Ed, who hardly talks at all. 'Me, I don't talk much, I just cut the hair.' This is true. Ed hardly mutters a word. Indeed, his decision to get involved in a dry cleaning business is on the understanding that he becomes the silent partner! Yet his internal monologue – which is the film's narration – makes him as loquacious as any Coen character. 'They're paying five cents a word, so pardon me if I've told you more than you wanted to know.' With almost his dying breath, he apologises for telling us his story.

Ed doesn't make an impression on the people he meets or on the audience. With the film's rather ambiguous structure and lack of closure, it is difficult to extract a moral from this tale, or indeed to divine quite how we are expected to feel about Ed, but that is in no small part because he is, with a few crucial exceptions, a completely passive passenger within his own narrative. In terms of the influence he can consciously have on events, he may just as well not be there.

This failure to conform to generic stereotypes led to a lot of reviewers taking the black and white photography as proof that the film is neo-Noir. After all, neo-Noir is the new black! But where is the *femme fatale*? You keep wanting Doris to be a *fatale*, but she's not. 'Big' Dave is in no better position than her husband to assist her financially. She just wants 'Big' Dave to open the annexe so she can become manager rather than bookkeeper. Her lack of ambition is hardly more exciting that her husband's.

As well as dwelling on the shadows of the urban 1940s, *The Man Who Wasn't There* is a critique of the sunny, suburban 1950s. Set on the line between the 1940s and 1950s, it carries the hallmarks of both decades.

Ed and Doris' house represents the acquisitiveness and conformity of 1950s America: 'The place was okay, I guess; it had an electric icebox, gas hearth, and a garbage grinder built into the sink. You might say I had it made.' Of course, Doris' conspicuous consumption of clothes and perfume eats up a lot of their income, but she does get it all at a 10 per cent discount.

At the core of the film, Riedenschneider stands in a pool

of intense light, subdivided by bars of Noirish shadow and discusses (in a vague and, it must be said, uncertain manner) Werner Heisenberg's Uncertainty Principle. This, at least as far as Riedenschneider is interested, demonstrates that 'Looking at something changes it.' This realisation, of course, undermines all of jurisprudence. After all, how can one rely on witness testimony if the very presence of the witness changes those actions to which they were witness to? You might as well find the witness guilty.

The two competing methods for explaining the ways of the world are the scientific explanation and the spiritual. As Riedenschneider has demonstrated, science has failed to come up with a coherent theory to explain Ed's predicament. Let's see how religion fares. When we see Ed and Doris together in the church, she is playing bingo. 'I doubt if she believed in life everlasting; she'd most likely tell you that our reward is on this Earth and bingo is probably the extent of it.' He goes along because he finds the church 'peaceful.'

This, as with many people, is the extent of his religion. But then Creighton Tolliver enters his life, and has an apocalyptic effect on Ed and his family that tests their complacency to its limit. Creighton Tolliver is the Devil character we have come to expect from a Coen film.

When he enters the barber shop, under the pretext of having his non-existent hair trimmed, his second line gives us our first hint: 'I wish I was doing well enough to turn away business... The public be damned.' He is here to tempt Ed. And Ed is only too keen to sign Tolliver's contract. And what for? Not for him the Faustian appeal of Helen of Troy, nor a return to youthful vigour. No, Ed is tempted to sign away his soul in return for a share in a dry cleaning business.

Goethe's Teutonic epic *Faust* looked at Alchemy, a process which is part Science and part Superstition, and showed the disparities between the two competing concepts. For

Goethe, the real danger was in smug self-satisfaction, in the absence of progress. In this respect, the stationary Ed Crane is fair game for Mephistopheles because he is pretty much a sitting target. It is also worth noting that Faust was also tempted by the child/woman Gretchen. Ed is tempted by Birdy and, as with his German predecessor Faust, no good comes of it.

Much later, when Ed wishes to make Tolliver accountable for the chaos his plan has made of his life, he returns to the hotel (not dissimilar, it must be noted, to the Hellish Hotel Earle in *Barton Fink*) only to find that the Devil has flown 'like a ghost... disappeared into thin air, vaporised like the Nips at Nagasaki.'

But, if there is a Devil, is there an Angel? Well, flying the flag for scientific logic over superstition we do have Freddie Riedenschneider, an ostensibly unlikely candidate were it not for one thing... that beam of Godly light in which he is framed while developing his Uncertainty Theory. He is there to offer a hand of salvation and redemption to both Ed and Doris if they are prepared to accept it. He is confident (and we have no reason to doubt) that he can save Doris from the chair. But her own guilt leads her to take her own life before he can save her.

As Ed begins to feel the stress of his guilt, complicated by his inability to save her by simply telling the truth, he turns to Birdy for relief. When Ed first meets the almost fully-grown Birdy, she is hesitantly playing the tune which has run throughout as Ed's theme: a slightly detuned, echoey rendition of Beethoven's *Pathétique* Piano Sonata. Birdy informs Ed that Beethoven was deaf when he wrote it. It seems fair, therefore, to assume he was uncertain about how it actually sounded.

As Ed listens with little comprehension to her uncertain rendition, he finds 'some kind of escape. Some kind of peace.'

This could be the same peace he found in the church, but he spoils it by lusting after Birdy... as Billy Bob Thornton so eloquently confesses on the DVD audio commentary 'Ed's got a boner!'

Families: Ed and 'Big' Dave have one big thing in common: their wives. They both married into their employment. In Ed's case this means he works in his brother-in-law Frankie's barbershop. In Dave's case, he is manager of the department store that bears his wife's maiden name. This means that neither of them truly wear the trousers in their houses. When Ed blackmails Dave, the money he is paid isn't Dave's, it's the company's, which Doris has helped him embezzle.

Doris' family, the Raffos, are prone to alcoholism, it seems. Doris disappears into a drunken stupor to cope with a family get-together. Frankie later follows suit when he can't cope with his sister's untimely death.

Dreams: As with the ending of *Barton Fink*, we find ourselves contemplating the conclusion of *The Man Who Wasn't There* and comparing it to the end of Terry Gilliam's *Brazil* (1985), wherein all that we see or have seen is but a dream within the dream. There are two points where Ed's recollections seem to slip into hallucination.

The most obvious point when the narrative slips away from reality is the car crash. We see this in slow motion to the accompaniment of Ed's comment: 'Time slows down before an accident, and I had time to think about things.'

He thinks about the spinning disc of the UFO which hides behind the clouds of 1950s paranoia, then he thinks back to a time before his wife's death... to a time of status quo in the Crane household. He imagines himself sitting on his porch and, for the first time, his house is not shrouded in shadows from the nearby tree. It is a glorious summer day. He watches his wife demonstrate her powerful and determined personality by rejecting the advances of a tarmac salesman. They don't want a new drive, they don't want to change, things are fine as they are. Indoors, they sit, silently, without looking at each other. Neither partner is actively involved in the marriage, yet this is the image Ed clings to as being the good old days to which he wished he could return.

And so he is dragged back to the life he had hoped to escape... Persky and Krebs, the cops who told him about Doris' arrest, are there to welcome him back to life. They lean over him and ask 'Are you there? Are you awake?' They are actually looking him in the eyes and they don't know he's there. He has resumed his traditional role of invisibility.

But is this real or another hallucination? We feel it's the latter. He imagines the scene underwater, with Tolliver's body being found. His burden of guilt over what happened to 'Big' Dave and to Doris is such that he now wants to be punished for anything. We never know what happens to Tolliver, so Ed ties up that loose end and gets himself blamed for it, because he quite clearly hasn't been blamed for any of the things he has actually done.

Riedenschneider employs his uncertainty defence, which turns on the notion that to prove something means you have to alter it and therefore make it wrong. The Coens' challenge to their viewers is... prove that all this isn't happening in Ed's head.

Finally, Ed's story ends as it began, with him tied to a chair in a sterile white room. Initially it was a barber's chair, now it is an electric chair. The image fades to white with Ed wondering once more if there actually is an afterlife.

Okay, so that, we think, explains the rather disjointed final reel, but we would also argue that Ed drifts into dream, and possibly insanity, far earlier in the film. In fact, the last moment which can definitively be thought of as real is the moment when he learns that Doris is dead.

After Doris' death, as he gazes up through the wire-frame roof of the courthouse elevator, he decides once and for all that there's nothing up there... only sky. He feels he is living in a Godless universe. It seems reasonable that, from this point onwards, he slips into insanity and everything we see is actually just his hallucination, a dream in which he explores his own motives. Did he want to deliberately destroy his unfaithful wife and usurp his brother-in-law? Was it really that simple?

Let's explore that in a bit more detail:

Among the first things he tells us after his wife's death is that her brother Frankie falls apart and Ed becomes *de facto* 'principal barber.' Yet this gives him no sense of an ambition achieved. As he walks home through a herd of slow-motion passers-by 'it was like I was a ghost walking down the street... I *was* a ghost; I didn't see anyone; no one saw me... I was the barber.' In its own quiet unobtrusive way, Ed's mind is spiralling out of control.

His way of seeing the world becomes more and more surreal and Roger Deakins' way of photographing it becomes correspondingly more stylistic. Previously the cine-matography had only been noticeably emblematic and Film Noirish during key scenes, such as the showdown between Ed and 'Big' Dave. Suddenly, Ed finds himself sharing a drink in a Noir bar with Dietrichson the country medical exam-iner (who is named in honour of Barbara Stanwyck's *femme fatale* in *Double Indemnity* [1944]).

Immediately after this, he briefly experiments with that afterlife idea, employing a bogus clairvoyant who puts him in touch with his wife 'Dolores.' Outside her apartment, there is a moody corridor and a gratuitous overhead shot of a backlit doorway, which is so Film Noirish as to be almost pastiche. This sudden change to an expressionistic cinematic style ties in with Ed's embracing of a more bizarre world – which includes, for the first time, mediums and even UFOs.

From there onwards he starts to rework the film's story, but this time he includes himself. He is no longer the man who isn't there. He gives himself a leading role in his own story. He goes to see Birdy and tells her he wants to help make her famous. He has 'made enquiries.' This is a phrase he has borrowed from the most hyperactive character in the film – Riedenschneider: 'They tell me the chow here's okay, I made some inquiries.'

He is trying to do something good, he thinks, to build a future for someone. He has entered the realm of wish-fulfilment, fuelled by his true (far less paternalistic) motive and the image of Birdy lounging across her bed, stroking her legs and agreeing to go to San Francisco with him.

Ed's imagination tries to derail his desires, with the surreal French maestro Carcanogues in his bizarrely ethnic studio who insists that Birdy's playing – rather like Ed – has no soul.

Immediately after this disappointment, he imagines that this child, over whom he has such mixed feelings, takes away the confusion for him by seducing him. So Ed grants himself his perfect death, the wish-fulfilment of his base desires and the blessed release from his guilt over his wife. But it isn't that simple. The car crash is his punishment for Doris and Dave. Surviving it to face conviction for a crime he didn't commit – a true rerun of his wife's story with him now as the main character – is his punishment for giving in to his desire for Birdy.

We therefore feel that everything from Doris' death onwards is really just Ed's nightmares, his self-inflicted mental punishment for crimes he casually or accidentally committed. Crimes for which no one else would convict him. After all, he couldn't be guilty; he wasn't even there.

Intolerable Cruelty (2003)
'Obscene wealth becomes you!'

Cast: George Clooney[2] (Miles Massey), Catherine Zeta-Jones (Marilyn Rexroth), Geoffrey Rush (Donovan Donaly), Cedric the Entertainer (Gus Petch), Paul Adelstein (Wrigley), Richard Jenkins[2] (Freddy Bender), Edward Herrmann (Rex Rexroth), Billy Bob Thornton[2] (Howard D. Doyle), Irwin Keyes (Wheezy Joe), Jonathan Hadary (Heinz, the Baron Krauss von Espy), Tom Aldredge (Herb Myerson), Bruce Campbell[4] (Guy on TV)

Crew: Director: Joel Coen, Producer: Ethan Coen, Brian Grazer, James Jacks, Sean Daniel, Writers: Robert Ramsey. Matthew Stone, Ethan & Joel Coen, Cinematographer: Roger Deakins[7]. Music: Carter Burwell[10], Editor: Roderick Jaynes[8]. Colour, 95 minutes

Plot: Miles Massey is a cock-sure divorce attorney, supremely confident that no would-be gold-digging divorcee will ever make a sucker of him, or any client he represents. Marilyn Rexroth is a would-be gold-digging divorcee. When her husband, Rex, falls off the tracks, it's full-steam-ahead to the divorce court. Rex enlists the aid of the wily Miles and, as a consequence, Marilyn that ends up empty-handed. This forces her to counter-attack the only way she knows how... after all, she may have lost the battle... but all is fair in love and war.

Commentary: The Coens return to the much-loved genre of the screwball comedy – with an emphasis on turning the screw – and provide us with a romantic comedy with nary a trace of romance.

Although *Intolerable Cruelty* is set in contemporary LA, its set and costume designs employ voguish retro-chic to put the perceptive viewer in mind of the 1930s and 1940s. Indeed, many reviewers, including Roger Ebert in *The Chicago Sun-Times* and Peter Bradshaw in *The Guardian*, have referenced the sophisticated screwball comedies of Lubitsch and Hawks; but the film to check out is Tim Whelan's 1938 British comedy *The Divorce of Lady X*. Laurence Olivier stars as a stuffy divorce lawyer, Logan, who has a very low opinion of women and marriage and is tricked by the unmarried Leslie (Merle Oberon) and the thrice-divorced Lady Meer (Binnie Barnes). Also, for the star turn of a con-woman trying to trap her rich hubby, check out Preston Sturges' *The Lady Eve* (1941) with Barbara Stanwyck and Henry Fonda. As with *Intolerable Cruelty*, the opening credits include Victorian cupids firing arrows of desire.

Miles Massey is a man in love… with himself. In *USA Today* Clooney describes Massey as the grandson of *O Brother Where Art Thou?*'s Ulysses Everett McGill, bearing the family traits of fast-talking self-importance undermined by a thick streak of vanity. We first meet him as a set of ultraviolet teeth (as lawyers are commonly likened to sharks – it's important to have perfect teeth), which are being artificially whitened whilst chatting to his secretary, who can understand every word despite the mouthful of dental paraphernalia, implying many such conversations. Thereafter he is frequently seen to be admiring his own enamel in any convenient reflective surface, including the back of a spoon… until Marilyn enters his life and becomes a whole new object of affection for him.

The casting of Catherine Zeta-Jones-Douglas as Marilyn

Rexroth-Doyle-Massey was an interesting coup for the Coens, as well as a brave choice on Ms Jones' part, given the criticism that some commentators levelled at her for marrying into the notoriously wealthy and powerful Douglas dynasty. One wonders if this satirical role was, for her, part of a charm offensive to win over Hollywood in time for the 2003 Oscars. If so, her Best Supporting Actor award for *Chicago* would suggest it worked.

Given its subject matter – the traditional Coenical contemplation on the lure of big bucks and the deals one makes to secure them – it is amusing, if not especially revealing, to consider that this is the Coens' first 'studio' film since *The Hudsucker Proxy*. It is also the first film, since *Hudsucker*, that they have not written in isolation. Instead, they have partnered up with glitzy Hollywood producer Brian Grazer (culpable for *A Beautiful Mind* and *How the Grinch Stole Christmas* among many other Ron Howard delights) to re-work a screenplay by Robert Ramsey and Matthew Stone which had been kicking around Hollywood for much of the 1990s.

The ever-unpredictable brothers presumably decided that the one thing they'd never done before was sell-out. So, with the guarantee of star names and a global distribution, this marriage of convenience produced a film about marriages of convenience. How very mischievous of them.

One of the major problems with this film is its literal demonisation of women. This doesn't begin with Marilyn's woman in red, but rather in the film's opening pre-title moments, when Donovan Donaly returns home to find his wife, Bonnie 'having her pool cleaned' by Ollie the pool man. When he reacts in the traditional American manner by pulling an (admittedly very small) gun, Bonnie emasculates him by stabbing him in the ass with his Daytime TV Lifetime Achievement Award – which just happens to be shaped like a devil's trident. She can be said to have nailed his ass.

Which brings us to what is, presumably, intended to be the yin to the film's misogynistic yang... its sniggering homophobia. This begins with Donaly's early trident-buttock interface, then continues with Miles' flippant suggestion that maybe Bonnie could claim that her husband was being unfaithful with the hired help. When he decides this is possibly a claim too far, he shrugs the idea aside... 'I'm not on a mission.'

But seemingly the Coens (or their co-writers) are: this is best exemplified in the monstrous shape of Gus Petch – who serves the essential Coenical role of screaming fat man, with his persistently bellowed 'I'm gonna nail yo ass.' He is the most homophobic character presented here. Yet, as is often the case with denial, his protestations would seem to disguise a strange fascination. As he inadvertently admits: 'My job is to nail asses, I'm an ass nailer.' Take that as you will.

His unfounded vanity over his physique would suggest a deeply repressed homosexuality, especially when seen in the light of his constant sexual allusions: 'I've always had ample proportions... private dick... pussy-foot' and the fact that his only interest in heterosexual sex seems to be in videoing other people doing it. The only glimpse we have of his home-life involves something akin to an all-male orgy, as his rogues' gallery of fat black friends watch his ass-nailing tapes with him – while his (presumed) wife is relegated to an off-screen voice.

If we turn the patent-pending homoscope toward Miles, we similarly find an (albeit subtler) subconscious interest in the love that dare not speak its name. When discussing the boredom of his all-conquering Alexandrian life – he mentions he has three 'yard men' (gardeners) and has 'a man who waxes my jet.' This elliptical interest in the hired help echoes Bonnie Donaly's sleeping with the Pool man, as well as Marilyn's friend, Sarah, enviously eyeing-up the naked, glistening flesh of her own yard man.

Even when Miles is displaying his masculinity to Marilyn, he still finds himself saying 'Like you, I'm just looking for an ass to mount.'

When he meets Howard Doyle, Miles is unflustered by the revelation that, at college, Doyle was a 'Tight end.'

Of course, there is the whole question of the sexual orientation of lawyers in general. Marilyn's is called Freddy Bender – and the Coens are sufficiently well-versed in English idioms to know what 'bender' means over here. Then there is the somewhat less than aggressively masculine Wrigley (a character who bears more than a passing similarity to Philip Seymour Hoffman's Brandt from *Lebowski*), who cries at weddings (all of 'em) earning the appellation 'Pollyanna', who buys Marilyn and Howard spoons for their berries(!), who feels that the signing of the Massey Pre-Nup is romantic ('Only love is in mind if the Massey is signed') and who delights in Miles' evocation of the exotic name 'Ten-zing Nor-*gay*.'

All of which does, admittedly, seem tenuous – were it not for the fact that lawyers, as presented in *Intolerable Cruelty* are, almost without exception, driven to destroy heterosexual relationships. So the presentation of homosexuality here is uniformly repressed and negative. With one conspicuous exception.

When the 'Tenzing Norgay' witness turns up – he is the impossibly flamboyant Heinz, the Baron Krauss Von Espy... a name so silly it needs repeating at least three times. He is the only unrepressed, openly gay character – and he is so outrageously, enthusiastically, unashamedly camp he seems to have almost evolved into his own unique life-form. As if his every signifier didn't broadcast his sexual orientation – Marilyn claps eyes on him and breathes the transparently familiar 'Puffy', confirming Miles' allegation that she spent a lot of time as a 'guest' of *La Pantalon Rouge* – 'The Red Trousers.' He's certainly an entirely new depiction of a person who is – for want of a more ennobling term – a pimp.

All this repressed homosexuality and implied homophobia aside, at least it can be said that the Coens are not shying away from lampooning a social group which is protected by discrimination legislation, as well as the single most litigious sector in society… lawyers.

Puffy Von Espy allows us to segue nicely into our next subject for consideration: the strategic use of dogs. Dogs have appeared before in the Coen's world, most obviously in the form of the Devil's bloodhound in *O Brother*, but here they are ubiquitous. Puffy has his pampered pup Esbetta, Marilyn has Howard, her unfeasibly fluffy poodle (which bites Miles the first time it sees him) and her rapacious rottweillers which lead to the most alarming sexual allusion in the whole film, courtesy of the thoroughly repellent Gus Petch. When he breaks into Marilyn's house at Miles' behest, he is set upon by these vicious and unusually intelligent dogs. He later describes them as having a 'hard-on for anus Africanus', a truly repulsive image, if taken literally, and no doubt a significant contribution to Miles' and Wrigley's fear of the dogs when they later break into her house.

Here, dogs really do seem to be man's worst enemy… well, straight man's, anyway. This, therefore underscores how far off-beam Marilyn is when she refers to Miles as a 'schnauzer', however this comparison between lawyers and dogs may cut to the heart of the film's attitude towards legal professionals. Yet, of course, it is these self-same dogs who save Marilyn and Miles' marriage by stopping Wheezy Joe in his tubercular tracks.

No Coen film worth its pillar of salt is without its Biblical undertones, and here we have the Devil incarnate – a woman scorned, clad in vivid red – who will possess Massey and make his head turn round. When Puffy discusses Marilyn's past – he refers to her wanting 'A man she could cuckold' and makes little devil horns with his fingers.

Yet, all of this seems positively divine when compared to the darkness at the heart of Massey/Myerson... the shrivelled homunculus of Herb Myerson, squatting in the dark of his Hellish den, seemingly kept alive by drips and machines. As Myles sits nervously in the ante-chamber of Hell, he flicks through the magazines and discovers, to his horror, a copy of that coffee-table classic 'Living Without Intestines.' This implies that Myerson isn't entirely human, certainly not entirely whole. In Myerson's office, epic religious choral music booms out, not unlike that listened to by Big Lebowski in his mourning chapel. Religious music in this damnable place... clearly the Coens are inviting us to look upon Herb, rather than Marilyn, as the Devil in the details of this particular tale.

Further undermining Marilyn's initially obvious claim to Deviltry is that fact that she isn't always in red. When she turns up for her first date she isn't in red and when she is court, she proclaims her innocence by wearing white, as she does during her mock marriage.

During their meal, Miles pointedly asks: 'I assume you're a carnivore.' And is told 'I eat men like you for breakfast.' (He wishes). She compares her pursuit of men to a hunter on safari not hating the animals. She wants money or independence and men are her way of getting it. Her marriages are a cold-hearted business transaction and, as such, she is a classic *femme fatale*. She may not be entirely red in her couture, but she is in tooth and claw.

After losing the case, she mixes her red and white colours and wears pink. After her wedding to Miles, the cushions on their marital bed are pink and white. After her (apparent) successful divorce of Howard Doyle, she flaunts her new worth by wearing gold. After successfully separating from Miles, she switches to black and white, uncomfortably evoking the ghost of Joan Collins' *Dynasty* days.

While the female characters wear their motivations on their designer sleeves, the men are characteristically less subtle. Their predilections are betrayed by the subtext within their dialogue. They pepper their dialogue with Freudian hints at their inner turmoil and true motives. When Miles is asked to give the key-note speech at the up-coming NOMAN convention (that's the National Association of Matrimonial Attorneys, Nationwide, of course, with its heart-warming motto: 'Let NOMAN Put Asunder'), he absently bats away tennis-balls while casually telling the caller that he will '…get right on it, I'll whip something up.' A reasonably innocuous statement, when not taken in the sexually heightened context of this film. We are constantly reminded that 'The Massey Pre-Nup has never been penetrated', while Miles modestly explains that he doesn't like to 'Blow my own horn.' When Puffy explains Marilyn's plan he characterises that it was to 'Make hammer on his fanny.' a.k.a: nail his ass, yet she is later told 'The Massey Pre-Nup has never been penetrated… You *can't* nail his ass.' Ironically, and not irrelevantly, Miles' NOMAN speech from the previous year was wittily entitled 'Nailing your Spouse's Assets.' Of course, the sexual miasma bubbling away just beneath the surface is not restricted to lawyers and their witnesses – the first plaintiff we see is the innocuous-looking Mrs Gutman who was her husband's 'sexual slave', save when he was in the Navy (note he wasn't in the Army!!). Upon his return, he fashioned her vacuum cleaner into 'The Intruder.' She prefers the tennis pro at the club – who she refers to as 'David and Goliath.'

More subtly, Rex Rexroth's great turn-on is trains, the

phallic nature of which is now enshrined in cinematic history thanks to Hitchcock's last shot in *North By Northwest*.

Even before this, we get Donovan Donaly with his phallic Jag (which his wife steals) his over-compensatory pony-tail and his tiny little pistol (which was actually his wife's).

Yet, curiously, in this landscape of loaded language and double-barrelled entendre – when Miles and Wrigley break into Miles' house, they protect themselves from Marilyn's marauding rottweilers with distinctly non-phallic aerosol cans.

Indeed, despite himself, Miles is very far from the thick-necked schnauzer Marilyn originally thought. He's a sensitive, sophisticated new man. He quotes Shakespeare's *Julius Caesar*: 'The fault, dear Brutus, lies not in our stars but in ourselves…' After he rashly kisses Marilyn, assuring her that it is a liberty for which he would be happily disbarred, she is genuinely impressed and accurately declares: 'A romantic attorney.'

It should, therefore, come as no surprise to us that he is eventually converted into a fully rounded human being by the time he steps up to the podium of the NOMAN convention to make his speech. There he stands, Miles Longfellow Massey, having achieved a full-on Capraesque epiphany, sans tie and looking somewhat shambolic – almost like Jimmy Stewart after a few days' addressing the Senate (or was it Congress? Who understands American politics, anyway?). He tears up his speech just as Marilyn had torn up the Massey Pre-Nup and, as she had stood before him 'exposed', he stands before his peers '…naked, vulnerable and in love.' His 'love is good' sentiment is, of course, a not-very-thickly-veiled allusion to the unfortunately famous 'greed is good' speech made by Zeta-Jones' real-world hubby, Michael Douglas in Oliver Stone's laughably limp *Wall Street* (1986). Talk about keeping it in the family …

Family: In rewriting the script, the Brothers Coen have surgically removed almost all traces of familial conviviality. A comedy about divorce lawyers must, perforce, concentrate its attention on failed or failing families and, as such, Wrigley and Miles make for the most consistently successfully family unit herein.

The distinctly effeminate and emotional Wrigley is the mother to Miles' distracted and temperamental father. Their clients are treated rather sternly or patronisingly, as inattentive parents might treat their children.

They debate Miles' boredom and his desire for a real fight, over the head of Mr Gutman, as though he weren't there, and their Abbot and Costello-style 'Have you sat before her before' routine with Rex Rexroth is simply a sarcastic parent having a joke at an earnest child's expense.

Ultimately – Freddy Bender and Wrigley fight like children over the Pre Nup, but all Miles and Marilyn the lovebirds hear, is the '…patter of little lawyer's feet.'

Dreams: Miles fears Herb because, if he isn't careful, he will become him, demonstrated overtly with Miles' nightmare, from which he awakes, rather like his spiritual ancestor, Ulysses McGill, with his hair all messy.

In a scene cut from the script, Miles confesses to his chess-partner, Kenneth (a character completely written out in subsequent drafts) that he fears ending up like Myerson 'With a colostomy bag instead of a family.'

Script Revisions: So, let us look in detail at some of the changes wrought by the Brothers on the script. Fair warning, the version from which we have compiled these notes is available freely, but unofficially, via the Internet and is therefore purely offered as a matter of interest rather than record.

There are some significant differences between the script

as shot and the script the Brothers inherited, written in 1997. Primarily, all the sympathetic female traits have gone, all hints of family and motherhood have been carefully removed:

Freddy Bender was originally Ruth Rabinow, a woman defending a woman.

Marylin (sic) was much less predatory – she had genuine affection for Rex and was devastated by his philandering.

Marylin's friends had children – which humanises them somewhat and makes them less self-obsessed. They were also seen in exercise class, rather than indulging in 'elective' surgery.

Puffy's role was originally filled by a woman called Patricia Kennedy Decordoba Isenberg Banderas – who happened to be Marylin's mother. By replacing her mother with her pimp, the Coens are insisting on a very different reading of Marilyn's character.

As noted, Miles' chess-partner, Kenneth has been completely written out. Much of his purpose in the script has now been adopted by Wrigley – who was only a minor player in the 1997 version.

When their divorce turns nasty – Miles had Marylin jailed, she, in turn, threatened him with the IRS.

The female judge was named Marva Munson. This name has subsequently been employed for the eponymous lady in *The Ladykillers*.

Bad Santa (2003)

'He doesn't care if you're naughty or nice.'

Cast: Billy Bob Thornton[3] (Willie), Tony Cox (Marcus), Brett Kelly (Thurman), Lauren Graham (Sue), Lauren Tom (Lois), Bernie Mac (Gin), John Ritter (Bob Chipeska)

Crew: Director: Terry Zwigoff, Producers: Sarah Aubrey, John Cameron and Bob Weinstein, Executive Producers: Joel and Ethan Coen, Writers: John Requa, Glenn Ficarra, Cinematographer: Jamie Anderson, Composer: David Kitay, Editor: Robert Hoffman. Colour. 98 minutes

Plot: Sleazy thief, Willie (Thornton), along with the help of his little friend (Cox) spend every December posing as Santa and his Elf in some garish department store somewhere – then, come Christmas Eve, this month-long recce results in a beautifully crafted night of theft, leaving them with enough moolah to live happily for the next 11 months. Except that this year, Willy unexpectedly finds the joy of Christmas.

Commentary: The wafer-thin basic premise: 'Bad' Santa's life is reformed by lonely fat kid (Brett Kelly), who in turn finds his voice (and his fist) through his friendship with Santa… is the kind of 'high concept' movie Governator Schwarzenegger would have made about 10 years ago, when his action–movie career first went into nose–dive. What saves this from a completely ignominious end is Thornton's rendition of Santa as a foul-mouthed, booze-swilling, cigarette-smoking, incontinent, promiscuous thief – whose first reaction to anything new is to punch it.

Surely there can't be many movies out there which include a scene of Santa having anal sex in a ladies' changing room. Well, not the sort of films one would bother to *write* about at any rate, since they're not typically watched by people who can read.

Bad Santa is undoubtedly lewd, crude but not without a certain roguish charm, especially for anyone who loathes those feel-good holiday movies. This is the perfect antidote to artificial Christmas cheer, as Thornton seems to relish ruining long-cherished traditions in his role as the micturating Santa. But special mention must go to the late John Ritter, as the department store's prissy manager, who fears a law suit on behalf of all little people when he contemplates firing the Elf, and to Bernie Mac as the corrupt security guard.

And, in case you were wondering… why have we included this in a book about the Brothers Coen? Well, they seem to have been given the grand title of 'Executive Producers' for coming up with the one-line 'high concept' pitch which was picked up by screenwriters John Requa, Glenn Ficarra *(Cats & Dogs)* and Terry Zwigoff *(Ghost World)*. They also apparently mentioned the resulting script to Thornton, for which I'm sure he will remain grateful, as the film will very quickly find its way onto the 'play once every Christmas' list.

The Ladykillers (2004)

'I smite, you smite, he smites... We done smote!'

Cast: Tom Hanks (Professor G. H. Dorr), Irma P. Hall (Marva Munson), Marlon Wayans (Gawain MacSam), J. K. Simmons (Garth Pancake), Tzi Ma (The General), Ryan Hurst (Lump Hudson), Diane Delano (Mountain Girl), Stephen Root[2] (Fernand Gudge), Bruce Campbell[5] (Humane Society Worker)

Crew: Director: Joel & Ethan Coen, Producers: Ethan Coen, Joel Coen, Tom Jacobson, Barry Josephson and Barry Sonnenfeld[4], Writers: Joel & Ethan Coen, based on *The Ladykillers* by William Rose, Cinematography: Roger Deakins[8], Music: Carter Burwell[11], Editor: Roderick Jaynes[9]. Colour, 104 minutes

Plot: A mad professor hatches a plot to rob a floating casino – by tunnelling into its safe from the basement of a rented house. The only two things that stand in his way are the spectacular incompetence of his carefully hand-picked gang, and the indomitability of his land-lady. If this sounds vaguely familiar – we refer you to the 1955 Ealing film *The Ladykillers* to which this film bears more than a passing resemblance.

Commentary: The Brothers Coen have always been masters at re-working tired genres – their takes on film noir, gangsters and Frank Capra sparkled with as much affection as inspiration. Their eye for the original was married with an irreverence that created genuinely fresh work, a very long way from the hollow 're-imagining' so prevalent, in lieu of genuine inspiration, in Hollywood these days.

These films were proper *homages* in that they remind one of the original, without being a slavish copy or a shameless burglary. So it came as some surprise when the rumours were confirmed that the Brothers would indeed be directing an actual remake of the film which many consider to be the definitive English comedy: *The Ladykillers*.

Some deemed this move blasphemous or ridiculous or just plain odd. The original was too closely identified with its time and place – being firmly located in post-war England – and with its quirky, clumsy, charming Englishness. Of course, the affection in which the film is held in England is not reflected over in the States. To them, it is not Holy Writ. Indeed, the multiplex crowd may not even realise it's a re-make.

When further announcements confirmed that the action would be transplanted from the North West of London to the Coens' beloved Deep South of America, and that the gang (still masquerading as a string quartet) would be after the loot from a Mississippi steamboat, hackles on this side of the Atlantic settled down somewhat. Given how charming *O Brother* had turned out, with its depiction of an alternate-reality-Deep-South almost, but not quite, entirely unlike the real thing, surely the Brothers would successfully oversee the transition. After all, if someone absolutely *had* to re-make an Ealing film, who *else* would you choose?

Well... not Tom Hanks, sadly. Whilst his performance as Professor Goldthwait Higginson Dorr PhD is a welcome and long-overdue return to comedy, and allows him to unleash a talent for eccentricity, which he has never really had the chance to unveil before, he seems at odds with the rest of the film.

True, his performance hardly resembles Alec Guinness' original at all (which is to the credit of all concerned) but it does have the same caricaturial breadth. He seems somewhat displaced in a film with a contemporary setting, since he bears the demeanour (and wardrobe) of a moustache-twirling silent movie villain of 80 years past. His exchanges with his equally eccentric landlady, Marva Munson, form the highlight of the film but, again, stand proud from the rest of it. There is something genuinely Coenical about this double-act, but the great shame is the film which surrounds them neither supports them nor sympathises with them.

Everything started so promisingly – up in the clouds, to the accompaniment of music – devotional music – which immediately puts one in mind of *O Brother.* We pan down and the idyll is broken by a gargoyle and a jet-black raven. An ominous foreshadowing of what is to come… after all, it's not a great stretch to go from Jack Daw to Dorr! Maybe this is the arrival of the film's demonic antagonist, in symbolic form. Certainly, this same raven assists in Dorr's passing on from this mortal world in the film's closing moments.

Many Coencoctions have a trace of the old Good Versus Evil buried in their subtext. But rarely has the spiritual aspect of their work risen so promptly or conspicuously to the surface. These early scenes are marinated in a deep spiritu-alism, a source of inspiration and instruction to Mrs Munson and all who have not the heart to argue with her.

She opens by complaining about a neighbourhood youth – Weemack Funthes – who has, in her opinion, imperilled his very soul by getting 'a blastah' to play his 'Hippety-Hop.' Consequently he is '…hanging by a thread over the Pit… the

Fiery Pit.' Her primary expenditure in life is the money she sends to a Bible School ('I'm an angel') and her primary occupations are discussing the ills of this mortal coil with her dead husband's portrait – or reading aloud from the Bible. It is during one such recitation that Dorr's shadow darkens her door: 'Behold – there is a stranger in our midst, come to destroy us.'

This particular Devil, rather like Marilyn Rexroth before him, is dressed in white. With his white cloak, Pan-like goatee beard and widow's peak, he looks traditionally demonic, yet he presents a whiter-than-white academic, intellectual façade. But she is far from being impressed by this charming man's long words. Noticing this, he changes tack, and informs her that his cover – the quartet – 'play… devotional music… church music.' And so we descend into the root cellar where the gang are all set to dig their own tunnel – their own Pit.

In church, the lesson is to guard against 'Worshipping the Golden Calf.' And there it sits, moored on the river bank – beckoning Dorr and his merry band of reprobates. And, further out in the river – an island of garbage which, the preacher teaches, symbolises the folly of the mortal world – 'this Earth' as he calls it. Well, Dorr and his colleagues will, in the fullness of time, be smitten down, leave this world and arrive in that one. Again, foreshadowing this inevitability, the 'band' arrive in their chosen mode of transport – a hearse – and set to digging through 'this Earth' to 'the golden calf' (cash cow) of The Bandit Queen.

References to earth and digging are reminiscent of the Snopes brothers rising out of the ground in *Raising Arizona* – and the escapees rising from the ground at the beginning of *O Brother*. Both of these moments were rebirths – characters springing anew from the good Earth from which we were all fashioned once upon a time. Here the villains are digging *into* the Earth, literally interring themselves. But then, *all* passengers in hearses end up underground! Earth to Earth and all that.

Another reference to G.H.'s status as something less than saintly and a man with less of a future than he may suppose: He reads books in 'so-called dead tongues' (the invocation of which is one of the defining characteristics of those supposedly possessed by demons). He also loves the works of Edgar Allen Poe which include, of course, references to ravens, premature burials and tell-tale hearts beating away beneath floorboards. Maybe this heightened awareness of the relationship between mortality and the earth is a Southern thing.

Either way, into this heightened, spiritualised environment, the ensemble assemble, bringing with them their profanity and their scatological (one could say *earthy*) humour, and perfectly epitomising why the disparate elements of the film simply don't integrate well into a coherent whole.

Dorr's dialogue weaves elaborate, lyrical pictures, heavy with excessive expression. But, upon closer inspection, he is generally saying nothing. Whilst he is the most overtly Coenical character in his disturbing eccentricity and love of the sound of his own voice, a loquacious imbecile makes for an amusing character performance (Goodman's Bible-selling Cyclops in *O Brother*, for instance) but is of insufficient substance to make for an engaging central performance. Nevertheless, in his own way, he is just as divorced from the real world as Mrs Munson, which explains why their exchanges are among the highlights of this film.

However the cronies with which Dorr surrounds himself are dull and listless compared to these two luminous creations. The gang conform to tedious basic stereotypes: Gawain, the bling-encrusted foul-mouthed black youth, the inscrutable Oriental shopkeeper known only as the General,

Lump the muscle-bound moron and Garth Pancake, the long-winded (emphasis on the *wind*) red-neck explosives (emphasis on *explosive*) 'expert.' Granted, their precursors in the original *Ladykillers* were no less clichéd, but at least Herbert Lom and particularly Peter Sellers brought some panache to their performances.

The opening moments of the Coens' rendition lull the unwary viewer into feeling that they are going to watch a dark, sophisticated comedy with immediate and obvious echoes of *O Brother*. Instead, one finds oneself watching flatulent slapstick almost entirely conforming to the voguish and infantile *American Pie* formula. It begins with CPR administered to a dog… and proceeds to spiral downwards from there.

Equally distressing is the absolute lack of drama – since the crooks are so incompetent there is never a moment when one feels they may actually succeed in either milking their cash-cow or killing the obstructive Mrs Munson.

Ultimately, the Coens' take on *The Ladykillers* makes for a charmless film, with plenty of dick and fart jokes, substituting the original's deadly black humour and the Coens' own trademark wit. The Coens' visual and verbal élan has transmogrified into ugly caricatured performances and crude mechanics. By taking on a masterpiece and up-dating through dumbing-down, they have, one fears, dug their own grave.

Family: Whilst Dorr's gang bicker like a family, his lack of control over them (neither the General nor Garth seem to pay much attention to his attempts to maintain parental authority and the youthful Gawain is entirely beyond his control) would seem to undermine this. Curiously, when Gawain gets his chance to fulfil the role of gun-toting gangsta he can't bring himself to kill Mrs M, because she reminds him of his mother. More intimate is Mrs M's relationship with her house… the wallpaper is very like the Earle in *Barton Fink*, which was more like skin on a living thing than paper on a hotel's walls. This, combined with the ever-changing portrait of her husband, Othar, goes towards making it seem as though the house is alive – or at least being guarded by a power from above.

Part of Mrs Munson's holy trinity – is her cat, Pickles. If the raven is Dorr's animal familiar, then Pickle's is Mrs M's. The cat is omnipresent, overseeing everything that transpires, and creating as much of a nuisance as possible. Ultimately, Pickles finishes them off by disposing of the only remaining part of their plan – Garth's lost middle digit. It is therefore safe to say that Pickles delivers our ultimate judgement on the film by giving the gang the finger.

Theater of the New Ear (2005)

Sawbones

Cast: Steve Buscemi[6] (The Coward Frank MacReady), John Goodman[5] (Jerry Nelson), Marcia Gay Harden[2] (Agnes Barley), Philip Seymour Hoffman[2] (Sawbones/Varlan Smith), John Slattery (The Salesman), Brooke Smith (Joan Nelson)

Crew: Writers and Directors Joel and Ethan Coen, Music: Carter Burwell[12] , Foley Artist: Marko Costanzo[1]

Hope Leaves the Theater

Cast: Hope Davis (Herself), Peter Dinklage (Himself), Meryl Streep (Herself)

Crew: Writer and Director: Charlie Kaufman, Music: Carter Burwell[13], Foley Artist: Marko Costanzo[2]

Plot: 'You're watching a movie, in a theatre or at home, and starting to doze. You can't keep your eyes open, but the sound of the film still seeps in through your ears, which sadly are never closed. Your mind paints the picture itself in that meaningful but not quite visual way that dreams play out. This is the experience I'd like you to have now.' Carter Burwell,

Theatre programme Notes for *Theater of the New Ear*
Original Sound Plays.

Commentary: It may have been Friday the 13th (of May
2005), but for some (2,600) people walking through the
foyer of London's Royal Festival Hall it was anything but
unlucky. They had managed to get tickets for the two sole
performances of *Theater of the New Ear*, original sound plays
performed by a who's who of indie film super-stars, all
crowded onto one stage.

The excitement in the Hall was electrifying, not only was
there the boggling on-stage talent, but sitting in the audience
before the lights went down, we had great fun celebrity spotting: Sir Paul McCartney and Heather Mills were further
down our row, Stephen Frears was looking down on us,
Jeremy Irons, Sinead Cusack and Cillian Murphy were also
spotted. Seeing Joel and Ethan Coen, Tricia Cook, Frances
McDormand and Charlie Kaufman trooping in to watch the
proceedings began to seem like a most natural occurrence.

As the lights dimmed, on walked the members of the
eight-piece band, the Foley artist, Marko Costanzo and
finally Carter Burwell (who in addition to working with the
brothers, worked on Kaufman's *Being John Malkovich* [1999]
and *Adaptation* [2002] as well as all the afore-mentioned
Brothers Coen movies) who conceived the event as well as
composing and conducting the on-stage octet. Then as the
stage lights grew brighter, out shuffled John Goodman, Steve
Buscemi, Marcia Gay Harden, Philip Seymour Hoffman,
John Slattery and Brooke Smith. All dressed in black they
stood, scripts in hand, behind their microphones and we were
off.

The first play of the night was the Coens' 30-minute play
Sawbones, which inter-cut a TV western of the same name,
with the lives of those watching it. Philip Seymour Hoffman

played the soap's veterinarian hero caught in a love triangle with a school teacher (Marcia Gay Harden) and his arch rival (Steve Buscemi). The avid watcher of the soap was housewife (Brooke Smith) who also finds herself in the middle of a love-triangle when she begins an affair with a door-to-door salesman (John Slattery), much to the chagrin of her fire fighter husband (John Goodman). The style of acting was deliberately melodramatic and over-the-top to match the pastiche TV western and the ridiculous climax to the off-screen love triangle.

Sadly, the combination of the actors' microphone technique and the play's break-neck pace left much of the dialogue incomprehensible, especially as their delivery was often drowned-out by the overly-enthusiastic band.

The highlight of the play (other than being only a few feet away from the line-up) was the fun of seeing behind the curtain, as it were, and watching the Foley artist creating all the sound effects live – from dripping taps to gunshots to the removal of a bullet from a person's leg.

But then, no sooner had it begun than it was over.

Interval. Please talk among yourselves. You may wish to fetch a drink from the fridge. No thanks, I'm driving.

And we're back.

Those familiar with Charlie Kaufman's eccentric *oeuvre* might have cockily thought that they were prepared for a live Kaufman experience – but oh, how little we really know of the man!

The houselights were still up when the band and Carter Burwell ambled back on-stage, followed by Hope Davis, Peter Dinklage and Meryl Streep. Sitting down on stools (obviously this play was going to be longer) they began talking while the audience drifted back in. The three actors on-stage were playing three members of the audience, having themselves returned from the bar. With perfect English accents, Peter Dinklage and Meryl Streep began talking about the play they (and we) had just seen. Then Hope Davis began to utter her internal monologue, as the third audience member.

As the play-on-stage began (featuring Peter Dinklage and Meryl Streep), Hope Davis continued her commentary about how pretentious it was and what on Earth was it all about. Peter and Meryl continued to flip back and forth between on-stage performers and audience members in typical Charlie Kaufman reality-bending fashion and, just as we in the real audience were getting the hang of its complex but hilariously funny conceit, a third layer of reality is introduced.

Streep stops being either the actress in the play or the audience member in the stalls and becomes a grotesque caricature of herself, bitching about her co-stars and the appalling decline of theatregoers' behaviour!

Peter and Hope listen in frustration to this tirade, before the plays begin again. Confused? Well it is Kaufman.

Like his films, the play captures the spirit of the bizarre world he creates. I could wax lyrical about his play for some time, delving further into the multi-layered piece and even the misleading list of characters and scenes in the theatre programme, but sadly as this is not the Pocket Essential Charlie Kaufman we'll have to leave it there.

The Royal Festival Hall performance was the only one in London, but the nine actors had performed the two plays at the St Ann's warehouse in Brooklyn, New York for three nights (from Thursday 28 April to Saturday 30 April), following a week's rehearsal period. One of these was recorded for Sirius Satellite radio (who helped finance the production) for broadcast that September. How well they will work on radio is debateable since both plays play fast and loose with the radio form and rely quite heavily on you recognising the performers, as well as admiring their performances. *Hope Leaves the Theatre*, for example, is a play about a play being performed in a theatre, whilst *Sawbones* is about a person watching a television programme.

Carter Burwell, quoted in *The Times* (30 April 2005), says: '...the actors are doing it for fun, they're attracted to its uniqueness... [and they are] relishing the rough and ready preparation.' It certainly sounds as they entered into the spirit of thing as they were paid the same fee ($6,000) and, out of that, had to pay for their own airfare and accommodation. If they ever come back, we've got a sofa bed they're welcome to fight over.

Conclusion

By the end of 2005, the Brothers had directing a five-minute segment for an experimental portmanteau film called *Paris, je t'aime* (*I Love Paris*) which aimed to weave together a series of disparate stories, one set in each of the Parisian *arrondisse-ments*. There are also unsubstantiated rumours about another remake of a British heist comedy – this time the 1966 Michael Caine, Shirley Maclaine vehicle, *Gambit*. Curiously, like *The Ladykillers*, this film featured Herbert Lom in a supporting role. Hmm...

So, the Dudes abide. We don't know about you, but we take comfort in that. It's good knowin' they're out there, Joel an' Ethan, takin' her easy for all us sinners. We sure hope they get back to making more personal films.

Well, that about does her, wraps her all up. Things seem to 've worked out pretty good for Joel an' Ethan, and it was a purt good story, dontcha think? Made us laugh to beat the band. Parts, anyway. Course, we didn't like seein' 'em adaptin' other people's work so much. But then, we happen to remember when the Brothers wandered off the trail a ways back, they returned with *Fargo*, which relaunched their careers. So, we'll see what they come up with next... Aw, look at us, we're ramblin' again. Wal, wuh hope you folks enjoyed yourselves. Catch ya further on down the trail.

Reference Materials

Reference Materials

Books

Robertson, William Preston & Cooke, Tricia (Ed), *The Making of The Big Lebowski*. Insightful and witty insider's view of the Coens' crazy world. Faber and Faber, 1998

Korte, Peter & Seesslen, Georg (Eds), *Joel and Ethan Coen*. Hilariously well meaning and po-faced. Almost translated into English from the original German by Rory Mulholland. Titan Books, 1999

Woods, Paul A (Ed), *Joel and Ethan Coen: Blood Siblings*. Useful gathering of previously published magazine articles. Plexus, 2000

Levine, Josh, *The Coen Brothers*. Witty and whimsical retelling of all the usual stories. With pictures. ECW Press, 2000

Bergan, Ronald, *The Coen Brothers*. Haven't read this one, so you'll have to make up your own mind. Orion, 2000

Robson, Eddie, *Coen Brothers*. Haven't read this one either, but other books in this series are very useful, we have no reason to expect less from this one. Virgin Books (UK), 2003

Articles

Ansen, D, 'The Coens: Partners in Crime,' *Newsweek*, 21 January 1985

Behrens, Michael A, 'Cinema Brats: The Coens and Their

Scripts,' *San Francisco Review Of Books*, 17 January 1992, pp 25-6

Billen, Andrew, 'The Billen Interview,' *Life*, 4 September 1994, pp 10-11

Biskind, Peter, 'The Filmmaker Series: Joel and Ethan Coen,' *Premiere*, March 1996, pp 76-80

Breitbart, E, 'Leaving the Seventies Behind: Four Independents Find Happiness Making Movies in the Manner of Hollywood,' *American Film*, May 1985

Cameron–Wilson, James, 'The Coen Bros.,' *Film Review*, December 1997, p 69

Edelstein, D, 'Invasion of the Body Snatchers,' *American Film*, April 1987

Ferguson, K, 'From Two Directions,' *Film Monthly*, February 1992

Francke, Lizzie, 'Hell Freezes Over,' *Sight and Sound*, May 1996, pp 24-26

Handelman, D, 'The Brothers From Another Planet,' *Rolling Stone*, 21 May 1987

Horowitz, M, 'Coen Brothers A-Z: The Big Two Headed Picture,' *Film Comment*, September/October 1991

Nathan, Ian, 'The Coen Brothers: Unplugged,' *Empire*, June 1996, pp 66-69

Pooley, Eric, 'Warped in America: The Dark Vision of Moviemakers Joel and Ethan Coen,' *New York Magazine*, 23 March 1987, pp 44, 46-8

Richardson, John H, 'The Joel and Ethan Story,' *Premiere*, October 1990, pp 95-101

Robertson, William Preston, 'The Coen Brothers Made Easy,' *Playboy*, April 1994, p 112(7)

Robinson, David, 'Brothers under the System's Skin,' *The Times*, 1 September 1994

Sharkey, Betsy, 'Movies of Their Very Own,' *New York Times Magazine*, 8 July 1990

Spinard, Paul, 'How Low Can You Go?' *Sight and Sound*, October 1998, pp 30-32

Zimmerman, Paul, 'Interview With Coens,' *The Film Zone Web Site*, 1996

Web Sites

The best web site to visit is Paul Tweedle's www.youknow-forkids.co.uk. Which is British. Makes you proud, doesn't it! It'll tell you everything all the others will, with most of the fact-free gossip removed. It has a very clear, easy to navigate design and has billions of links to every other Coenical site you'll ever need. There is even a tantalising glimpse of what is (possibly) to come from the Coens in the future, at www. youknowforkids.co.uk/futureprojects. Start campaigning now – we *must* see *Jesus Quintana: The Second Coming*!

Scripts

Blood Simple & Raising Arizona by Joel and Ethan Coen, Faber and Faber, 1988

Barton Fink & Miller's Crossing by Joel and Ethan Coen, Faber and Faber, 1991

The Hudsucker Proxy by Ethan Coen, Joel Coen and Sam Raimi, Faber and Faber, 1994

Fargo by Joel and Ethan Coen, Faber and Faber, 1996

The Big Lebowski by Ethan and Joel Coen, Faber and Faber, 1998

O Brother, Where Art Thou? by Ethan and Joel Coen, Faber and Faber, 2000

The Man Who Wasn't There by Ethan and Joel Coen, Faber and Faber, 2001

Collected Screenplays: Blood Simple, Raising Arizona, Barton Fink and Miller's Crossing Faber and Faber, 2002

Short Stories

Gates of Eden: A Collection of 14 Stories by Ethan Coen, Doubleday, 1998

Gates of Eden Audio Book Much of the above, read by John Goodman, John Turturro, Steve Buscemi and William H Macy. Simon & Schuster Audio, 1998

Poetry

The Drunken Driver Has the Right of Way by Ethan Coen, Crown Publishing Group, 2001

DVDs (UK Region 2, unless indicated)

Blood Simple – Director's Cut Region 1 (B00005LC4P) Extra: 'Hilarious' Fake Commentary.

Raising Arizona (05191DVD 20th Century-Fox Home Entertainment) Extra: Trailer.

Miller's Crossing – Special Edition (01852DVD) Extras: Barry Sonnenfeld Featurette, Interviews with Gabriel Byrne, Marcia Gay Harden and John Turturro, Still Gallery, Trailer.

Barton Fink Region 1 Extras: Eight Deleted Scenes, Still Gallery, Trailer.

The Hudsucker Proxy Region 1 (B00000ING2) No extras, dammit.

Fargo Special Edition (17279CDVD) Extras: 'Minnesota Nice' Documentary, Coen Brothers Interview, Roger Deakins Audio Commentary, *American Cinematographer* Article, The Coen Brothers Repertory Co.

The Big Lebowski (OSS0702 Universal Pictures Video) No extras but there is a 33-page booklet! Woo.

The Big Lebowski Region 1 (6305165912) Extras: Cast and

Crew Biographies, 'Making of' Featurette, Trailer and TV spots.

The Big Lebowski Collector's Edition. This wasn't available at the time of writing, but had Christmas 2005 market release dates set for Region 1 and 2. Quite what features would make this a 'Collector's Edition' were yet to be confirmed, however www.youknowforkids.co.uk reported that there would be a box set edition to be called the 'Achiever's Edition Gift Set' which would include a bowling shammy towel, coasters decorated with photos and quotes plus a collection of Jeff Bridges' anamorphic photos.

O Brother, Where Art Thou? 2-disc set (MP014DS) Extras: 'Soggy Bottom Boys' Music Video, Post-Production Featurette, Storyboard to Screen comparison, 'Making of Down From the Mountain' Featurette.

Down From the Mountain (MP122D Momentum Picture Home Entertainment). Extra: Trailer.

The Man Who Wasn't There (EDV9138 Entertainment in Video) Extras: Genuine Commentary by the Brothers Coen and Billy Bob Thornton, 'Making of' Featurette, Interview with Roger Deakins, Deleted Scenes, Trailer, Photo Gallery.

Intolerable Cruelty (8206826 Universal Pictures Video) Extras: A Look Inside, The Wardrobe, Outtakes.

The Ladykillers (D881408 Buena Vista Home Entertainment)

The Coen Brothers' Collection Includes the Region 2 debuts of *Blood Simple: Forever Young*, and *Barton Fink* with the deleted scenes, *The Hudsucker Proxy*, and *The Big Lebowski* with the featurette.

The Coen Brothers' Collection Region 1 Contains a slightly different line-up of films from the Region 2 version – namely *Blood Simple: Forever Young, The Big Lebowski* Collector's Edition, *Intolerable Cruelty* and *The Man Who Wasn't There*.

DVD prices are so variable we won't bother quoting any. A good general rule, however, is that web sites are often cheaper than the high street. So, for Region 2, check out Play, Sendit (formerly Blackstar), Amazon or eBay. For Region 1, we'd suggest PlayUSA, Loaded 247, CD Wow, DVD Pacific or, again, eBay. We don't necessarily endorse any of these sites (until such time as they pay us to do so) but they're a good place to start. Shop around.

Index

Index